VICTORY
OVER
REJECTION

Applying the Victory of Jesus to Rejection, Fear and Social Anxiety

AMY HAYWARD

DEDICATION

This book is dedicated to Jesus Christ.
By His grace, for His glory.

The mature children of God are those who are moved by the impulses of the Holy Spirit. And you did not receive the "spirit of religious duty," leading you back into the fear of never being good enough. But you have received the "Spirit of full acceptance," enfolding you into the family of God. And you will never feel orphaned, for as he rises up within us, our spirits join him in saying the words of tender affection, "Beloved Father!" For the Holy Spirit makes God's fatherhood real to us as he whispers into our innermost being, "You are God's beloved child!"

ROMANS 8:14-16
The Message

CONTENTS

PREFACE

This is the book that I looked for when I was at my lowest point—I knew rejection was my biggest problem but I had no idea how to get to higher ground. We can spend so much time and energy trying to fight a battle on our own, when there are brothers and sisters in faith who have taken that ground and can share their wisdom and experience to help us get breakthrough a lot faster than we would on our own.

That is my prayer for this book, that others could learn from my mistakes, that someone just starting out in life could take hold of the victory that Jesus has provided a lot sooner than I did. I want my ceiling to be your floor, I want you to take hold of these truths and apply them so that you can get on with all that God has planned for your life.

The truth is, rejection is not really a giant that we need to conquer, but a distraction that we need to move past. The enemy uses rejection not to simply reject us, but to keep us from the amazing plan of God for our lives. You see, the enemy is so much more confident than we are of this: the Lord has prepared great things for us. There are assignments, adventures, and fulfilling relationships available to us that will transform this world. Rejection is one way the enemy distracts us from partnering with the destiny that our good Father has for us here and now.

What would be different in your life if you no longer feared rejection? How would you look five years from now if you walked into every room with confidence in your identity? What actions would you take if you knew just how loved you really are?

If any of your answers are different from your current reality, I believe this book will benefit you. You are worthy of the time and energy it takes to explore the truth about the rejection you've experienced. You are worthy of every moment of effort that it took for me to write this book. This world needs you.

ACKNOWLEDGMENTS

Thank you Sandra, Karin and Erika for being the midwives to the birth of this project. I could not have done this without your prayers and support. Thank you Haley for your editing talent— this book is much easier to read because of your contribution! Thank you to everyone who has supported me throughout the years and has been in my corner through all the ups and downs. We were built for community, and there's nothing I could create that would be the same without my community.

ENDORSEMENTS

"I've really enjoyed working through this book, written by someone who has lived what she is writing about. As a friend, colleague and co-worker of Amy Hayward, I have actually seen and sometimes participated in the journey that you will read about. Likewise I have joyfully experienced and observed the transformation that this author so openly shares with you in *VICTORY OVER REJECTION*. This book is important for those that have experienced or are experiencing rejection, just as much as it is for those who haven't. It is important for you who need to see and understand those who quietly suffer, and it is important for you who need to, at long last, believe that regardless of circumstances, you are not rejected but LOVED. It's all here, in 11 wonderful chapters that can take you from realization to transformation. If you're willing!"

Jon Buller
Juno Nominated Recording Artist and Pastor

"What I love about Amy is that her words in this book are not based on theories—they were born out of real-life experiences! She has sat with Him, been transformed by Him, and now led by Him. *Victory Over Rejection* is an incredible guide to freedom and identity. I highly recommend this book as well as the treasure of Amy herself."

Gabriel Lopez
Revival Group Pastor, Bethel School of Supernatural Ministry

"I had the privilege of reading this book and want to encourage anyone who is wrestling with rejection or ministering to others who do to get a copy and immerse in this rich, Bible-saturated work. Amy writes with a vulnerable, open heart. Her story and the principles she's learned and embraced will encourage and equip you to do battle and win against this common challenge we face as followers of Jesus. I also encourage parents and grandparents to understand these principles and pass them on as they teach and disciple their families."

Daren Wride, 12Church.com
Author, DNA of a Christ Follower

1

Rejected or Accepted

There was a fisherman who was out in the waters off the coast of the Philippines who encountered some bad weather. His small fishing boat ran into trouble when it got stuck on a rock off the shore, which almost destroyed the boat and the fisherman too. When he finally got his boat free, he took that rock home with him to remember how what had started as a traumatic incident, had been turned into a victory. This rock was about two feet long and one foot wide and weighed 75 pounds.

After his trip, this fisherman was tired and didn't know what to do with the rock. It was quite large and cumbersome, and didn't exactly make for a great display piece. Or so he thought. After sticking it under his bed, he ignored the rock for ten years.

When he was moving house a decade later, he was cleaning and packing and rediscovered the rock. It was at this point that the fisherman realized his rock was not actually a rock at all, but a pearl. With a little cleaning and a proper assessment, he learned that this rock he had been sleeping on was actually the largest pearl ever discovered and was worth over one hundred million dollars. This 75 pound pearl has been dubbed "The Pearl of Puerto" and is currently on display in the city hall.

This almost missed miracle will bring a life-changing windfall to the fisherman who discovered it, and will change the life of his family as well. The very thing he was sleeping on, the symbol of a difficult moment, was a transformation waiting to happen.

Rejection can be like this pearl—a difficult moment from our past that is a transformation waiting to happen. We might be sleeping on it, ruminating on our old wounds and not seeing the valuable potential. This fisherman might have stopped fishing altogether, scared of hitting another rock.

Maybe you have stopped trying to build relationships because it just feels so dangerous. But when we are willing to change our perspective and get some help, we will see incredible value in the very area where we have been stuck.

The very thing he was sleeping on, the symbol of a difficult moment, was a transformation waiting to happen.

The moments of rejection that we experience are compounded by the number of times we relive them in our minds, and they form our thoughts, actions and habits in the future. That's the problem with rejection, it's not so much about the one incident, but as it is about what it forms in us and the fear that we live in as a result of it.

Rejection opens the door to many other challenges and mindsets, strongholds that we label as personality types and fears that we welcome as means of protection. It becomes so ingrained within us, especially when we have early childhood events that set the stage for us to partner with rejection. For most of my life, rejection was my closest friend, my most familiar enemy, and so entangled in my mind that I couldn't even imagine myself separate from it.

I knew that it wasn't serving me well, and I envied people I knew who walked into every room with confidence. I had friends who seemingly had zero social anxiety and even found joy in events that only felt terrifying to me. I saw the distance between them and I, the stark contrast of their joy and confidence versus my fear and anxiety, but I attributed it to my circumstances. Their beauty, their gifts and skills, their acceptance in every room were the reasons they could be so confident and free. I was sure that if they were rejected the way I was, they would be just as upset and afraid as I was. What I wish I could tell myself then, is that their freedom from rejection had nothing to do with their circumstances and everything to do with what was going on inside their heads.

What if it is possible to separate yourself from those fears, those thoughts, and even the feeling of being rejected? What would it look like to live free from rejection, free from social anxiety, and no longer relive your worst moments?

Let's start by looking at the best example for every problem in life: the person of Jesus Christ. We only have a small glimpse of His life on earth, how He navigated the culture and community that He dropped in to—a few stories from His childhood, and some highlights from His last three years on earth. But Hebrews 4:15 tells us that He is not unable to sympathize, but experienced every weakness and temptation that we face, I love this paraphrase from the Message:

"Now that we know what we have—Jesus, this great High Priest with ready access to God—let's not let it slip through our fingers. We don't have a priest who is out of touch with our reality. He's been through weakness and testing, experienced it all—all but the sin. So let's walk right up to him and get what he is so ready to give. Take the mercy, accept the help."

Hebrews 4:14-16 The Message

So what help can Jesus offer us when it comes to rejection? Does He promise that we won't have to face it? Sometimes in the circles of Christianity that we build, there is a narrative that says we expect to sail through life, loved and accepted everywhere we go because we are following Him. We begin to think we should be never feel rejected and only experience optimal circumstances. But that's not quite what Jesus promised us.

One day we will be there, with Him where there are no tears and no pain, optimal circumstances and experiencing love and acceptance everywhere we go. But here and now, we are living in the in-between. The now and not yet kingdom, the seemingly conflicting reality that we are seated in heavenly places and walking on earth. We are not yet living in the utopia of Heaven, in the absence of all evil. We are living in a broken world, with broken people, and our enemy is out to steal, kill and destroy.

That is the not yet part, but the now part means that we have the Holy Spirit living inside of us, we are living in the victory of Jesus life, death and resurrection. We are in a unique season in the span of history where Jesus has already come and conquered, and we are living out that victory until He returns and the enemy is ultimately destroyed. It means that there should be evidence in our lives of the victory of Christ, that though we are surrounded by a broken world we actually have light and life inside of us.

If you think about it, the first Christians—the early church and the Apostles—were facing some really challenging circumstances. And they also had the Holy Spirit living inside of them. They looked different than the world around them. The now and not yet. The same reality that Jesus walked the earth in is the one that we are living in now. If He faced every temptation that we do, then that includes the temptations to fear, to doubt, to crumble under rejection and abandonment. He was fully God and fully man, navigating the inner reality of living with the Holy Spirit and the physical reality of interacting with broken humans and influences of an invisible enemy.

Jesus was everything that we should love and accept—perfection embodied and love personified. He lived without sin, never making a lapse in judgement or speaking without consideration. He never spoke or acted without love, and yet He was rejected again and again. This right here should take some pressure off of your shoulders. You will never be able to live so perfectly that you can stop people from rejecting you. You cannot perform your way into acceptance or protect yourself from rejection by being loving enough, kind enough, or perfect enough. You cannot control your way to being loved. Jesus lived perfectly, and He was rejected.

In fact, I would venture to say that He was more rejected than anyone else who has ever lived. When we think of Him now, we know that He is the Messiah, the Son of God, the Chosen One and the Saviour of the world. However, most people alive at the time did not think of Him that way. They thought of Him as a carpenter, as a local teacher, as another in a long line of prophets, or perhaps even a crazy nut.

His disciples, the ones that lived and worked with Him, the ones that saw Him do amazing miracles and got to look in His eyes every day, even they didn't really get who He was until He was gone. Do you see the number of times Jesus asks them, who do you say that I am? It's not because He's needing reassurance, and Jesus never asks a question He doesn't already know the answer to. It's just like way back in Genesis, when Adam and Eve are hiding in the garden and God asks "Where are you?". Questions from God are never a search for information, they are always an invitation for us to examine our answers.

The Messiah was inviting them to partner with truth, inviting but not demanding. He was claiming His identity as the Son of God, not hiding it by any means. He would get up in the Temple and proclaim His identity. But notice that Jesus was completely comfortable with being misunderstood. Even His closest friends were allowed to have their own idea of who He was even if they were wrong. He invited them to truth, but never tried to control their response.

In fact, He knew his disciples would deny Him as He died on the cross for their salvation, and He still moved towards that cross. He even humbled Himself and washed the feet of the men who were about to reject him. "Peter, you will deny Me three times"... I would have been more like Peter! Don't deny me! See who I am, I'm doing this for *you*! Peter don't be a jerk! But Jesus, knowing this great betrayal and rejection from His friends, still invites them to the garden. Allows them to join Him that night even though He knew they were fair weather friends.

And let's not forget Judas' betrayal, the ultimate rejection that leads to His crucifixion - do you think Jesus didn't know this was coming? Of course He knew, and I believe He knew before He chose Judas as a disciple. He knew at the last supper, when He broke bread and blessed it and passed it to the one who would betray Him. It's almost as if the rejection of other people, even His closest friends, had no effect on His actions.

One place in Scripture where we see rejection affecting the actions of Jesus is when He attempts to do ministry in His hometown of Nazareth. When the people there were offended by Him and did not believe He was the Messiah, He was unable to do any miracles for them. He didn't get angry, He didn't curse them, He didn't reject them or try to pay them back for the way they were treating Him. He simply respected their decision to reject Him and invested somewhere else. You could say, it was their loss and not His. That's something we say to each other, "Well if they don't want you that's their loss." It is true though, isn't it? It was the loss of Nazareth that they couldn't accept the Messiah.

What about family? Family is often a source for rejection for so many of us. If Jesus experienced every weakness and temptation that we have, did He also experience rejection from His family? Absolutely! We see this in the gospels that the whole time He was ministering, His siblings wouldn't buy what He was selling. They didn't believe Him until after His death and resurrection. If anyone should have been able to testify to the truth of who He was, it would be the people that had spent decades in close proximity! And yet they denied Him too.

The Scriptures don't actually tell us much of anything about what Jesus felt, only what He did. I wonder if that is on purpose? Maybe feelings aren't as important as we make them out to be. I'm sure Jesus felt the pain of all this rejection, but it didn't change what He did. Other people didn't have the ability to affect His actions, they could only place limits on what they themselves would receive from Him.

Jesus had a source for His identity, security and acceptance. He was focused on the opinion of His Father, and that was the voice He gave the most weight to. He didn't need to correct every voice that spoke something different, and He didn't panic when people exercised their free will.

Let's circle back. Jesus asked other people who they thought He was repeatedly. Why? Because it changed the core of the person He was asking. When you are confident of the identity of Christ, it transforms how you see yourself. Jesus asked this question not to elevate Himself, but to invite others in. If Jesus Christ was standing in front of you now, asking "Who do you say I am?", what would your answer be?

Your answer is the starting point for your own transformation, for your freedom from everything that is broken in this world. You see, if we believe Jesus is the Saviour, if we know Him as our friend and love Him truly, whether it's been mere hours or a lifetime, we cannot help but be changed. The reality of who Jesus is is greater than the reality of your circumstances. When you know Him, you become like Him. When you know me, nothing amazing happens. I mean, you'll have a good time and all, and hopefully be encouraged, but it's not going to transform your life. Knowing Jesus is a unique experience that changes your past, present and future.

If there is anyone who has ever had a good reason for people to accept Him, it is Jesus Christ. He literally provides salvation, healing and deliverance to those who accept that He is the Son of God. And still, He was unconcerned when people rejected Him. I'm sure it was hurtful: I'm sure His heart was bruised, but rejection did not steal anything from Him. We don't see any stories in the gospels where Jesus is rejected and it ruins His day. Or when people deny who He is and He re-evaluates His life goals because of it. We don't see that Jesus' friends reject Him and then He no longer has opportunities or a calling. Rejection does not steal from you, but your reaction to it will.

Let's take a look at some of Jesus' most personal rejections, rejections that would have thrown most of us off course. Probably the most obvious one is Peter. At the end of Jesus' life, we see Peter's betrayal, rejection, and abandonment of his friend Jesus. He had just promised Jesus that he would never deny Him, and then he turns around and denies Him not once but three times. Jesus saw it coming, and did not do anything to try to stop it. He had absolutely zero interest in controlling Peter's acceptance or rejection of Him.

The reality of who Jesus is is greater than the reality of your circumstances.

I have been in a similar situation, where a close friend promised me that they would not walk away, then turned around and walked away in a dramatic and hurtful fashion. I saw it coming, and I did absolutely everything I could to try to control the outcome. I was terrified of the potential rejection and when it happened I thought, "Well there you go. I knew it all along," and promptly spiralled into a deep depressive hole.

Jesus reacted quite differently, didn't He? This rejection from His close friend, this extreme betrayal that He saw coming, came true in a dramatic way. His response was to walk back in to Peter's life, cook him a nice breakfast on the beach and bring complete restoration. We see the fullness of restoration in this friendship too—Peter rejected Him three times and wept around a fire, and Jesus brought him back to a fire and invited him three times to affirm their love.

Let's look at another one, Judas. It's easy to see Judas as the bad guy: on this side of history, he is clearly a villain. Trading in our Messiah for a mere 30 pieces of silver - less than $200 in today's economy. But let's get out of the habit of villainizing people, and ask what Jesus might have seen. Jesus saw Judas as not only a disciple, a man that He trusted enough to share meals with, but as a friend. He saw him as someone He could trust with the authority to minister in His own name.

And remember, Jesus knew ahead of time the failures these men would have. He knew in advance what was coming, and it did not change how He treated these men. In fact, He even chose Judas to be the treasurer! The one who would sell him out for a few pieces of silver was the one Jesus looked at and thought, "Yes! He's the one I want to be in charge of the money bag". Jesus remained completely unaffected by the rejection of others. The betrayal of others did not change His ability to love and even empower other people, and there was no fear in Him.

If Jesus was consumed by the fear of rejection, we would've seen Him distancing Himself from Judas and Peter from the beginning. We would've seen Him put some high walls around them, or even attacking them out of anger. We would have seen Jesus refuse to invite Peter to breakfast after His resurrection. It seems as though rejection was a reality for Jesus, but not a factor in His decisions or His actions.

Let's look at one more example, John the Baptist. John was Jesus' cousin, and cousins are often our first friends. In fact, John was the first one to recognize Jesus for who He was. Remember when Mary and Elizabeth were both pregnant, and baby John leapt in the womb when Mary and Jesus entered? It's because he recognized the identity of Jesus. We don't see the full history of their relationship in Scripture, but we do see how John gave his life to preparing the way for Jesus and His ministry. John the Baptist was the one shouting out for people to repent because the Messiah was coming. He literally spent His whole life proclaiming the truth about Jesus, until the end of his own life, when things aren't going so well.

John runs into some fierce opposition and is jailed for his bold proclamations and ministry. With everything stripped away, John starts to question the identity of Jesus. He second-guesses his own declarations, asking "Surely if He is who He says He is, my circumstances would be better?" Maybe you can relate, I know I can. John hits a really low point, and questions who Jesus is. He begins to reject His friend, His cousin, His Saviour. The one person Jesus knew His whole life, who was supporting Him and speaking well of Him. The one He thought would always be by His side was now doubting Him and believing lies. John sends word from prison, asking if Jesus really was the Messiah. Imagine how painful that was for Jesus to hear. Even John the Baptist was doubting who He was.

I love the response of Christ here. When His prophet, His friend and cousin starts to question Him, Jesus responds by reminding John to look up. John was so focused on what Jesus *wasn't* doing, on his less than ideal circumstances, that he lost sight of what Jesus *was* doing. Many times, when I start to get discouraged and begin to doubt, Jesus reminds me to look back at what He has already done for me in my past, and see the blessings that I do have in the present. Even in difficult circumstances, there are things we can be thankful for because God never changes, even when our circumstances do. Focus on who He is, not what you would like Him to do for you next.

If Jesus was faced painful circumstances, and cutting rejection (and He did!), He can be a model for us of how to face those realities and not be defined by them. He did not live in fear of rejection, even though it would make a lot of sense if He did. I can't tell you how many hours I've spent imagining the worst case scenario occurring, allowing ultimate rejection to play out inside my head. I lived this way for years, anticipating rejecting before every social gathering, every event—every time I left my house. And those were pretend scenarios which rarely ever became reality. This kind of imagining sent me spinning into a spiral of depression and anxiety. It would cause me to pull away from everyone I knew, isolate myself, and set up impossible hoops for people to jump through before I would trust them in any way.

Frankly I was miserable to be around, because I interpreted everything as rejection. If I walked with friends into a movie theatre and ended up being the one sitting on the aisle, I would interpret that as no one wanting to sit next to me. I would assume that they didn't actually want me to come, and would spend the whole movie wondering if I should just get up and leave. I would agonize over what I had done wrong and what I could do better to get them to accept me.

I've also literally had people ask me to move to the end because they truly didn't want to sit with me. Rejection is not always in our heads; it is often a reality of living in this broken world. When I did feel rejected, my instinct was to isolate myself. My thought process re-instilled my belief that because I'm not wanted, it's best to be alone. I was convinced it was a win-win. Other people didn't want to be with me, and if I was alone I couldn't be rejected and hurt again. In a small way, I was able to control the pain by isolating to avoid it. You could say I took the Hagar approach.

We see the story of Hagar in Genesis 16 and 21. She was the female servant of Sarah, Abraham's wife. As a slave, she was in no position to assert any rights. Hagar was there to serve and to do as she was told. Her story gets really tough when Abraham decides that God needs some help coming through on His promises. He was getting nervous about God being late, and decided to help Him out. If you can relate, raise your hand and join the club. We tend to judge these characters in the Old Testament, but I don't see anything here that I haven't done a time or two.

So Abraham "helps" God by sleeping with Hagar to produce an heir. Sarah is agreeable at first; she wants to see God's promise fulfilled and figures this might be the only way. Sarah maybe thinks she is taking the high road, but her heart can't handle the repercussions and she reacts with bitterness and anger. Also very relatable. Just because we know what the proper reaction should be doesn't mean our feelings will always cooperate.

Hagar, remember, is somewhat of a victim here. She's serving this family, and then is told she needs to serve by being intimate with Abraham and becomes pregnant. Then her blind obedience brings anger from those she's trying to serve. Hagar is rejected by both Abraham and Sarah and runs away. I don't see anyone in this story I can't relate to, but this reaction to rejection is especially familiar to me.

Isolation is a natural reaction of our flesh when we are hurt. It's a clear and simple way to protect yourself from being wounded again. The unfortunate thing is that it's the exact opposite of what our spirits need in that moment. What Hagar needed was reconciliation and a safe place to raise the son she had been burdened with. She was wounded in family, and she needed healing in family. Just like Peter rejecting Jesus around a fire, he needed reconciliation around a fire.

The place of our wounding is often the very place God will pour out healing, and when we isolate ourselves from it we are in turn rejecting the healing God is providing. If you were wounded by your father, or mother, it is the Father heart of God, or the mothering heart of the Lord that is where your healing will come from. But if you decide to never get near a father again, you are cutting yourself off from the place of your healing.

Hagar ran away to the wilderness and pretty much gave up on life, for her and her son. Not just once, but twice. The beautiful thing is that God met her there. Remember, this was not God's plan. God's plan was to bring Abraham and Sarah a son through their intimacy, and for Hagar to serve them and be part of their family.

In all their brokenness, they created quite a mess, but God came in and blessed them anyways. He sent an angel to encourage Hagar, to call her back and restore her, and even to bless the child she was carrying. Years later, Hagar is once again rejected and finds herself alone in the wilderness. Things were still messy and broken, and she was hopeless and ready to die, again. And again, God meets her there, restores her and provides for her. He renews His promise over the life of her son. Hagar was rejected, her worst fears came true, and even when she didn't handle it well, God met her in the middle of it.

The place of our wounding is often the very place God will pour out healing.

God is not scared of our messes and mistakes, He has actually planned for them. One of His names is Jehovah Go'el, it means Lord my Redeemer. Redeeming brokenness is literally who He is. In Isaiah, we see that it's not only His identity but it's ours as well; we are known as His Redeemed.

> *"And they shall be called The Holy People,*
> *The Redeemed of the Lord;*
> *and you shall be called Sought Out,*
> *A City Not Forsaken."*
>
> *Isaiah 62:12*

Whose choices has your life reflected more when it comes to rejection—Hagar's despair and self-isolation, or Jesus' confidence and consistent love? Both were rejected, but it affected them differently. If you feel more like Hagar, can you imagine what it would be like to live like Jesus? How would your life be different if you were not taken out by rejection and constantly trying to manage it in your life? Take a moment to consider what your life could look like.

As we see from the life and example of Jesus, living free from rejection doesn't mean that we need to isolated ourselves from all relationships that could be hurtful. He did not try to control or manipulate the people who were rejecting Him. He remained open to love, had healthy boundaries, and while He experienced rejection, it had no power over Him. That is because the fear of rejection was never given a foothold in the life of Christ. When you are not living in fear of rejection, you're able to love people freely and recover from relationship wounds a lot easier. Through Christ we see that rejection is not our problem, but the fear of it is what will destroy lives and keep us from seeing victory.

2

Fear of Rejection

Online dating has become commonplace today, allowing people that wouldn't ordinarily cross paths to meet and build relationships. I've done my share of free trials on dating websites, hesitant and secretly at first, not wanting to admit that I was willing to talk to strangers online in an effort to find romance. The worst part of it for me is the endless small talk through keyboards, trying to discern through words on a screen if this person is a match. I prefer to skip to a coffee date, because that's where I can feel the connection and see if there is real potential. There's just so much room for misunderstanding when you're trying to build intimacy through emails and messages.

I remember one particular gentleman who contacted me

after seeing me on a dating site. I had turned off my profile at that time, in my stubborn refusal to pay for potential dates, so this guy had to take some intentional steps to track me down and reach out. We exchanged a few messages, and pictures as well. After a few basic exchanges, including photographs, I replied and asked the guy if he would like to meet for coffee.

Remember, he reached out to me, had already seen my pictures, and had searched me out. He had to work to find me at that time, so he was clearly interested. But for some reason, something went sideways in our communication. He heard something that I wasn't saying: he made assumptions based on other experiences he had or fears that were larger than life. As soon as I asked him out, he gave the strangest response. It was something along the lines of, "That's nice, but I'm sure you're not really interested, so don't worry about it." And I never heard from him again.

Even though I had shown an increase in engagement, it was interpreted as rejection. The interpretation he came to was quite literally the opposite of what was happening. This may sound silly or that there must be some other explanation, but I read and re-read those emails, looking for any other context for this turn of events. I wanted to find another explanation, but I immediately recognized this as the fear of rejection. It was a familiar friend for me, so when I saw it in someone else, I completely understood what had happened. This man had been rejected before, and the fear of it happening again was re-writing his reality in real time. There was no rejection in our relationship, but his fear of it actually caused him to reject me.

The very thing he hated was what he partnered with, and it robbed him of an opportunity. That is something we can all relate to! I've done it many times myself, and I'm sure you have experienced this as well. We need to clearly see how the enemy is using fear to steal from us, because we are responsible for what we know. Once you're aware of these strategies, you must change your habits, thoughts, and actions to be in agreement with what God says. Rejection is a very real event that is painful and difficult. It is out of our control for the most part, and is a reality a lot of us face. Rejection can steal from your past, but it is the fear of rejection that steals from your future. Both of them can affect your present state of mind, and knowing how that happens is a key to freedom.

The very thing he hated was what he partnered with, and it robbed him of an opportunity.

There's been a number of scientific studies over the last decade or two that look at how rejection affects our brains. For example, there was a study in 2003 at UCLA[1] where they had people play a virtual reality game where a ball was being passed between people. With VR goggles on, they could see 2 other people and the ball being passed to them.

As the scientists measured their brain activity through an fMRI scan, the other people in the game stopped passing the ball to the person being observed, continuing to play but rejecting the subject. What the scientists saw was that the brain responds to social rejection the same way it does to physical pain.

When you experience physical pain, there are specific parts of the brain that tell you where the location of the pain is coming from. Other areas are responsible for processing the feeling of pain, the unpleasant sensation. This is the anterior insula (AI) and the dorsal anterior cingulate cortex (dACC), the same areas that

---

[1] https://pubmed.ncbi.nlm.nih.gov/14551436/

lit up when the person was rejected in a VR game of catch.

These scientists have proven that rejection really does feel like a slap in the face. To your brain, they are the same thing. Our brains are really good at remembering rejection. It is a lot easier to remember emotional pain than physical pain—for example, you can remember stubbing your toe and that it hurt, but you don't re-experience the pain every time you remember.

Years ago, I was building a swing set in my backyard, and the large wooden beams that were not yet secured crashed down on my back and head. It was one of the most painful injuries I've experienced; I remember not just the sudden impact but the days and weeks of recovery where my body was in constant pain as well. I can remember how it affected everything I did—sitting, standing, even lying down. Everything had to be adjusted to accommodate the effects of the injury. But when I think about that injury, I cannot recreate the feeling of the pain. I remember it without re-experiencing it. I'm sure by recalling your own most painful moments, you would agree that remembering emotional pain is more traumatic than remembering physical pain.

In fact, if you so much as look at a picture of someone who has rejected you, it will trigger those same pain areas of your brain to light up. If you look at a picture of a past physical injury, nothing lights up. When you remember rejection, you are literally re-experiencing it, and that's why ruminating on the past can be so damaging.

As you are reading this, you probably have a bottle of Tylenol in your cupboard somewhere, and you know to take a pill or two when you have a small physical injury. If you have a headache, you reach for Tylenol. UCLA's scientists found back in 2003 that popping a pain reliever pill actually helps for emotional pain as well. In participants who were being reminded of rejection they had experienced, they found that taking a pain reliever actually helped. Now I'm not suggesting you stock up on pills, but let's be aware of how our brains work!

Your pain is real, your response to it is valid, and it makes sense that you want to avoid rejection in the future. If you put your hand over an open flame and get burned, it is logic and wisdom that prevents you from putting your hand over the flame again. Avoiding pain is not weakness; it is wisdom. However, when it comes to emotional pain, we need to slow down and examine the process we are in and make deliberate choices about what we want to do next. Often when we are trying to avoid emotional pain, fear is our motivation. Recognizing what is motivating us is a great place to start.

Rejection Sensitivity Dysphoria (RSD) is starting to be recognized by mental health professionals, and is characterized as experiencing an overwhelming emotional response to real or perceived rejection. RSD often appears as anger, negative thoughts, hopelessness, low self-esteem, heightened anxiety, depression and suicidal thoughts. The learned behaviour for people with RSD is perfectionism, people pleasing, and isolation. The dysphoria part of this title refers to the misinterpreting of social cues, like the potential date I was trying to connect with.

I know when I was at my lowest points, I had an uncanny gift for interpreting everything as rejection. I assumed the worst about everyone around me—people I loved and wanted to be connected to. Someone could look me in the eyes and say "Amy, I love you," and I would have a dialogue in my head, imagining how they felt like they had to say it, but it wasn't really true. I told myself that actions are more important than words, and so it really didn't matter what was said to me, I would be watching for some small action to tell me you were walking away.

I had learned that rejection was around every corner, and I would be a fool to not prepare for it. *Fool me once, shame on you, fool me twice, shame on me.* After feeling rejected by family, friends, work and church, I considered myself an expert in spotting rejection from a distance. You wave at me at the wrong angle from across the parking lot? I see you rejection, and I will walk away before you have the chance to hurt me again.

I'm a very logical person, and I much prefer to see things as black & white. Grey is messy, ill-defined and hard to control. Black & white is simple, predictable, and clean. When things don't make sense to me, I wrestle them down until they do. I'm so grateful to live in the Age of Google, because I cannot tell you how many times a day I Google something just out of curiosity. Why would you ever sit in the discomfort of not knowing when just about any answer can be found with a few clicks? This isn't a new thing for me though, it's not about the technology and information that's available now. Growing up, I remember we had a full set of encyclopedias that were well used. They lined the shelf in our basement, and I felt such safety in knowing that if I heard about something that I didn't understand, I could just look it up. Sometimes I would read them just for fun. Yes, I'm that kind of nerd.

With my high value for truth and logic, I was stuck in a pattern of justifying why rejection was so prominent in my life. I had so much proof! You could not tell me that rejection wasn't real, or that it wouldn't happen to me again. That's often what would happen though, well meaning and sincere friends would try to comfort me by telling me I hadn't actually been rejected, and that it would not keep happening. We would have friendly arguments about whether or not what I had experienced was actually rejection.

Sometimes people will try to convince you your pain is not real because another person didn't intend to hurt you. But intention is not the only factor, the action has effects regardless of the intention. Knowing someone's intentions is definitely helpful, and we should make space to understand each other.

But your emotional pain cannot be judged by other people—the truth is perceived rejection and actual rejection have the same effect. Regardless of whether or not it is justified, you have to recognize and deal with the pain it has caused. My logical brain could not accept those encouragements from friends who wanted me to just not see it as rejection.

I also had compiled so much proof from my history that I allowed it to define my future. When I had friends who tried to tell me that it wouldn't happen again, it felt like they were lying to me. I would think to myself, "You don't know the future, you can't promise me I will never be rejected again!" And because I knew from my past that it happened often, it seemed only logical to assume that the pattern of rejection would continue indefinitely. My value for my circumstances was so high that I was allowing it to rule my life. I had decided that my circumstances and feelings were the most valuable information, and they got to define what was true.

The problem is, that is not the same value system that God has. In the Kingdom, truth is the Word of God; truth is Jesus Christ Himself. God is not denying your circumstances and your feelings, He just does not give them the highest value. His Word is true whether we feel it or not, and His Word is true whether other people act in agreement with it or not. His Word is just true.

We are called to have the same value system that our Father does, to adopt His priorities and His thoughts, which requires us to recognize when things are in opposition to them. This is something we should be growing in our understanding of, and this is what it means to take our thoughts captive. Our greatest problems come when we let our thoughts run unfiltered, and we often justify that by using the "proof" of our circumstances and our feelings. Feeling rejected does not give you permission to start thinking things about yourself that are in opposition to what

God says about you. Somebody else actually rejecting you still does not give you permission to have thoughts in your head that God does not have in His.

Let's take a look at one of my favourite books in the Old Testament: Job. The only way I've ever heard this book taught in churches is in reference to suffering. We use Job as the great example of a man who loses everything and still trusts God. When I studied this book, I saw something in addition to the suffering. The book's introduction actually gives us a great clue as to what the author is trying to communicate. We see a dramatic scene where Satan enters the presence of the Lord and makes an accusation. The accusation of our enemy is that we are fair weather friends of God—we will turn from Him when our circumstances are not good. He is out to prove that we will hold our feelings and our circumstances at the highest value, and allow them to affect our identity, and our relationship with the Lord.

We are called to have the same value system that our Father does, to adopt His priorities and His thoughts.

We see in Job that his plan actually works really well. As soon as things change for Job, he and his friends ask the almighty *Why* question. They start asking God why this is happening, and when God doesn't answer, they begin to answer it for themselves. I would like to suggest that when we are asking God a question and not hearing any response, it might be because we've started with the wrong question. In our culture we like to say, "There's no such thing as a bad question," but I believe in our relationship with the Lord that there is sometimes a better question.

We love asking why because we crave understanding. In general, we are curious creatures who are uncomfortable with mystery. Why is the question we most often ask, and it's usually the wrong place to start. Most of us get stuck at the Why question and never move any further. Why is the wrong place to start because it's usually coming from a place of distrust. The Why question says, "This doesn't match who I thought God was, so I need an explanation." If we really trust His character and His Words, we don't need to ask why. From a place of trust, we can assume that God is still good, no matter what is happening or what we feel, and we can ask a better question like What ("God, what are You doing in this situation?"), or Who ("God, who do You want to be for me in this situation?").

Because Job started with the Why question, he wasn't getting an answer. And when we're not getting an answer, it's really tempting to fill in the blanks. That's exactly what Job's friends do: they fill in the blanks of the answer God was not giving them. They came up with all kinds of reasons why Job must be suffering, and then they attempted to act on those answers. Misdiagnosis always leads to disaster. They started with the wrong question, created the wrong answer, and acted on it.

The result was that Job was in a worse condition than where he started. 38 chapters later, after Job's friends try to fill in every blank for him, God shows up and finally responds. Only He does not address the Why question, but instead He tells them Who. Who God is, His character and His vast greatness, His power and His love, even though Job's circumstances and his feelings stood in contradiction to this. Both were true, but one has higher value. The Who question is more valuable than the Why, and reprioritizing the questions we ask must be a habit that we cultivate in our lives today.

If Why is more valuable to you than Who, you will be in an endless cycle of battling thoughts that lead you down a dangerous path. Trying to figure out why you are being rejected and how to prevent it might feel like a clear and practical solution, but it is one that is devoid of the presence of God. This is the goal of your enemy in this world: to get you to give feelings and circumstances a higher value than the presence of God. He is doing whatever he can to shift your attention and affection from Heaven to Earth. It is this kind of focus that gives the enemy authority in your life and allows fear to grow. The thoughts that you entertain are the outcome that you are feeding.

The term self-fulfilling prophecy is not a religious term, it is recognized by psychologists as the phenomenon in which an individual predicts a certain outcome and aligns their behaviour with that outcome. It is widely recognized that when you believe something will happen, you act in agreement with your belief and therefore influence the outcome, whether it be positive or negative. We see how this influences our relationships when we begin to believe that we will be rejected.

This fear of future rejection influences our behaviour, and we begin to act in agreement with it and actually influence the outcome. Our negative thoughts become behaviours, and behaviours affect our circumstances. When we fear rejection, we agree with it and it becomes a partnership. We end up in a covenant with the very thing we are trying to avoid and get away from.

So what is our alternative? We must start by redirecting our attention. Whatever we fear we give power to, which is why there are 100 different Scriptures that talk about the fear of the Lord. Letting God have His rightful place on the throne of our hearts means that we don't view anything as higher than Him. When we fear the Lord, we do not believe that rejection is more powerful than God's love in our lives. We do not put anything above Him. If we are not afraid of rejection, the power is taken away from it.

Without the fear of rejection, you may still be rejected, but it will not be controlling other areas of your life.

Whatever we fear we give power to.

For most of my life I was consumed with the fear of rejection —I had agreed with it for so long that I had given it power over me. It controlled so many aspects of my day that my thoughts were focused on it constantly. I had given this fear so much space in my life, and I felt truly powerless against it. It felt like a stronghold that was impossible to take down, an enemy with no weakness, a heavy ball and chain around my ankles that caused me to trip over myself constantly.

So I did what I could to manage it. That's what we do, right? We adapt and make exceptions so that we can just make it through a single day when things are this tough. I looked for small ways I could feel in control again, since I had given so much control over to this fear. Controlling my body, controlling little habits and routines made me feel safer and more peaceful. It also grew into controlling other people. I wouldn't have called it that at the time...I thought I was just surviving. I thought I was protecting myself because I believed no one else would. I thought I was being honest and vulnerable about my emotions, but a lot of the time I was subconsciously using those emotions to get people around me to behave in a certain way.

I was missing a key point—control is a softer word for manipulation, and that is what I was engaged in. It is not pretty to admit or talk about, but this is the reality I had to face. It was not until the day I started to call it what it is that I was able to change. Softening sin by giving it another name is giving it permission to stay.

Manipulating people and circumstances is another way we

rebel against the Lord. Do you notice that it's not at all like Him? God values free will so much that even though He always knows better and understands more than we do, He lets us make our own choices. Even when the stakes are really high, He lets us make our own choices. Even if it hurts people He loves, He lets us make our own choices. This all knowing, all powerful, immutable God of the Universe never once manipulates us. Even back in the garden of Eden, with a little bit of control (manipulation), God could have easily done a couple of things.

He could have built a fence around that tree. He could have appeared when the snake did and shown Eve the truth. He could have done a few small things that would have prevented the fall of man altogether and changed the course of history. But that's how high His value is for free will. That's how deep His love is for us—love allows people to make their own choices and does not try to control them. Instead, who is the one in the garden who manipulates? It's Satan of course. He twists words and makes suggestions... He doesn't even really lie to them, he just uses the truth to accomplish his own desires.

Controlling other people and how they respond to us is outside of our authority and we do not have permission to go there. It is rebellion. It always comes from a place of fear, even when we label it as love. Sometimes when we are attempting to control other people, we call it love because we do love that person and want them to succeed. But control (manipulation) is rooted in fear. If you're interested in learning more about this distinction, I highly recommend Danny Silk's books, *Keep Your Love On* and *Loving Your Kids on Purpose*. He does a great job of laying out healthy boundaries and how to stay connected without manipulating or partnering with fear.

Instead of trying to control rejection, we need to control our thoughts. We are encouraged throughout Scripture to control our thoughts, to take captive the thoughts that don't actually agree with our beliefs and to choose carefully what we give ground to in our minds and hearts. We actually get to choose our thoughts, and we'll talk more about this later in the book. What's important to recognize is that fearing rejection has a domino effect that results in a tangled mess of other problems that will take up all your energy and time. The fear of rejection is actually faith that you will be rejected, and faith always yields fruit.

It is a hard cycle to break, because the more you fear rejection, the more you will see rejection, and the more justified your fear will feel. Rejection can rob your past, but the fear of rejection will rob your present and your future. It will take over until you are consumed with fear and anxiety and are disconnected from others and from the Lord. We cannot change the wounds we have received or what other people choose to do, but we do have authority to take back our thought life, to live in peace, and to stay connected to the love of God in every situation and circumstance. If you have found yourself partnering with this fear of rejection in your own life, the first step in taking back that ground is to explore the areas in your life that have triggered rejection, and allow the Lord to expose those roots and heal them. Full healing is possible, and the Holy Spirit is a genius at it. You can trust Him.

3

Types of Rejection

It's important to be aware of the areas in our lives where we are vulnerable to rejection. Most of us first experience rejection at some level in childhood, and those wounds are hard to forget. They also position us to look for it as teens and into adulthood, and as we have seen, when the fear of rejection grows, it becomes a self-fulfilling prophecy.

In this chapter we will take a look at some of the different kinds of rejection one can experience, as well as the common outcomes of those specific types. When we look at the bigger picture, we can see the patterns and strategies the enemy is using to try to hold us back. Sometimes it's easier to see in some one else's story before you can recognize it in your own.

A story found in Genesis 37 that shows us what it's like for someone to be rejected by their family. Joseph of course–the boy with the dreams and the coat of many colours. Joseph, who was his fathers favourite and had a pretty great life. For perhaps the first time in his life, Joseph experiences rejection in an extreme way. He's 17, with a worldview that was full of hope and promise. Although, not everyone around him felt the same way. He had a gang of brothers that were jealous of the favour on his life, who were probably tired of his optimism and decided to do something about it. His brothers conspire against him to get rid of him, to make sure he's not a part of the family anymore. They didn't really care what happened to him, as long as he wasn't bothering them anymore.

Jealousy fuelled this rejection, and justified as it might have felt it was still wrong. Joseph had been unfairly favoured by his father, and had no hesitation in displaying that favour in front of his brothers. When they had the opportunity, they acted on their plot to get rid of him. Determined to kill their younger brother, they throw him into a pit and strip him of his colourful robe, the symbol of how their father favoured him. When compassion strikes one of the brothers, he convinces them to not kill him but leave him in this pit, and let the caravan of nomads do with him what they'd like. Joseph is scooped up by the strangers and taken into slavery, and he faces a grim future with a long, hard road ahead of him.

This event is only part of the rejection he faced: the final blow is when his brothers lie to his father, telling him Joseph is dead and should be forgotten. They convince him to not even look for his beloved son. His father wept and mourned, but never investigated or searched him out. Joseph was rejected, and abandoned by everybody he had ever known and loved. Joseph was alone.

We know from Scripture that his story turned around, that the Lord fulfilled His plan for Joseph's life and was faithful to His promises. Even when his enemies seemed to gain the upper hand, God used it to bring incredible redemption. For 20 years, Joseph lived out the process of moving from traumatic rejection into restored redemption. He had a promise from God, a dream where the Lord showed him that he would be respected and honoured by his family. This dream was in stark contrast to his circumstances, and he had to wait two decades before he saw it fulfilled.

When I read his story, I see that Joseph had incredible patience, peace, and persistence. He was able to overcome rejection, and it didn't control his life. Even an extreme story like his was not a lost cause, and it means that that same turnaround is available for us too. Our circumstances might be different, our stories have different beginnings, but we serve the same God. And our God never changes: He is the same yesterday, today, and forever. Wherever you've experienced rejection in your own story, God wants to turn it around and use it for good. We have to start by taking an honest look at where we're at, and then we need to invite Him to be the Author of our story.

Familial Rejection

Rejection from family can be confusing. It is often a mixed message—there are some indications of love and affection but there is also abuse, neglect, abandonment, or rejection. Rarely is there purely malicious interaction and completely negative dynamics in a family environment. We are complex human beings, and even when a parent is trying their best, they will make mistakes. Likewise, when a parent is overcome with challenges and negative patterns, they still love their child and have moments where that rises to the top.

These mixed messages are confusing for an adult to navigate and make sense of, never mind a developing child. A child might have a parent who says "I love you", but also abuses them, which unintentionally teaches the child that love looks like abuse. Or it could be that a child is abandoned by their father, and the mother does her best to make up for it. The love of the mother will never be enough to repair the rejection of the father—that child will find full healing in the love of their Heavenly Father. There are unique roles that each parent fills in a child's life, and when one is absent there is a wound that only the Lord can heal.

Wherever you've experienced rejection in your own story, God wants to turn it around and use it for good.

It can take years just to recognize that there were unhealthy patterns and behaviours in your home growing up—we need to be kind to ourselves as we begin to recognize and process those dynamics. Usually when a family has some of these damaging dynamics present (abuse, neglect, abandonment, rejection) they begin during childhood.

Even temporary circumstances that present these dynamics can be traumatic and have long lasting effects. If a child is living with one parent for a short amount of time, or if a new family member is visiting the home—these temporary situations might be short-lived but when abuse and damage is part of the picture, the child will deal with those effects for years to come. When there are more people involved and longer time periods of living under these conditions, the effects are compounded.

It's important to note that rejection is almost always an element of abuse or neglect, but abuse and neglect are not always present when there is rejection. If you experienced rejection, it does not necessarily mean you were abused. Regardless of whether or not abuse and neglect are also part of your story, your experience of rejection is still a valid experience and worthy of the time and attention to pursue healing and restoration.

There are a myriad of ways one can be rejected by his or her family. There is no all-encompassing definition or list of criteria that needs to be met. If love is withheld, has conditions, or the child's need for love is not met, there is an element of rejection, whether it is intended or not. Rejection doesn't have to be malicious to qualify as rejection. If one family member rejected you, but the rest were all pretty nice, it still counts. Our goal is not to explain, excuse, or justify the wounds we received as children in our family of origin. Instead, we want to identify them and address them, so we can begin to heal.

Rejection can be passive, aggressive, passive-aggressive, or perceived. The differences between them are about the intention of the person rejecting you, and they don't really change the process for healing or how you can move forward. Whatever way you were rejected or abused as a child; it was not God's plan. It was not your fault. Children are innocent—not perfect, but innocent. There is nothing in you or about you that caused or invited that treatment; there was nothing inherently wrong with you.

God's plan for family is that it would be a safe foundation. He designed us in community, for community. He planned for us to be born into a family, a group of people that are diverse but have common ground. People that will love each other unconditionally, protect, provide and encourage each other along the way. Families were meant to be places where we are free to grow. Families were meant to be safe, and parents were meant to be the safest people in your life.

Whatever your experience was as a child, you consider it

"normal" until you see enough evidence to the contrary. As children grow, they are constantly processing information and develop beliefs that help them make sense of their experiences. If you are rejected by your parents, you might make sense of that by adopting a core belief of "I am unloveable" or "I am unwanted".

Familial rejection will also affect the self esteem of the child, their self image, and how they relate to others. Since the parents were supposed to be the primary safe relationships for the child, when rejected, the child learns at an early age to not trust people or other relationships. This is when rejection starts to affect the peer and social relationships.

Social Rejection

Social rejection can begin at any age but for most people is linked to childhood experiences. In most school environments, any child that is seen as "different" is rejected in some way. Bullying, antagonism, ridicule and alienation are all forms of rejection. In todays world, a lot of rejection happens online in social media and messaging. Teens growing up in this world of advanced technology have to face rejection and social dynamics constantly, even if you turn off your phone you know people are still messaging each other or sending pictures.

There is something to be said for the good ol' days, when bullying from classmates happened on playgrounds and could be escaped. It still had devastating effects, but there were times you could feel relieved from it temporarily. For teens who are being rejected, there are often two paths of response: aggression or withdrawal. Social rejection has the same effects as familial rejection, causing the rejected one to develop core beliefs to explain their experience.

As an adult, social rejection is also a possibility in work

environments and social groups. If you experienced rejection in childhood, you will be prone to see it quickly as an adult. Unfortunately, as adults we can continue some of the negative habits we had as children, like seeing anyone who is different in a negative light. In a work environment, there's usually one oddball. We might subconsciously reject these people out of our own discomfort. Even in Christian environments, or should I say especially in Christian environments, we tend to judge each other pretty harshly. Judgement is a precursor to rejection, and they follow each other closely.

When adults are rejected, they are more aware of the event and what a socially accepted response is. In most cases, a rejected adult learns to hide their hurt and respond appropriately. This leads to a lot of withdrawal and isolation. Adults who have experienced ongoing patterns of rejection will have a strategy to defend themselves, and avoid future pain.

One of the good things about the advanced technology we have today is that it gives people an opportunity to find people online who are enough like them that they find a group where they are accepted, even if every social circle they have in their physical life has rejected them. While these online social interactions can be helpful, they are not sufficient in replacing in person relationships and each of us need to pursue connection in our daily interactions as well.

Romantic Rejection

Romantic rejection can be particularly challenging to process, as it is often directly tied to our self esteem and sense of worth. When we think of romantic rejection we think of being told no when asking someone out, or being dumped by a romantic partner. Most of us have a story or two about "the one that got away", the person we pursued but did not reciprocate our affection or attention. These are painful memories, and can be part of the normal human experience. There are also some situations where the rejection is particularly cruel or poorly delivered, which causes the emotional pain that hangs around and opens the door to the fear of rejection.

Another type of romantic rejection is being rejected while you are still in a romantic relationship with someone. This is confusing and painful, and takes time to work through. Sometimes a partner might withhold affection or intimacy, hide the relationship from other people, demean and emotionally abuse - these are all forms of rejection that continue in an unhealthy pattern until one or both partners make a change. When you are engaged in a relationship where this kind of rejection continues long term, it has long lasting consequences.

Most people respond in one of three ways - either becoming a victim, an aggressor, or retreating. It's the classic fight, flight or freeze. When we are under attack, whether it is physical or emotional, we default to one of these 3 responses.

Fighters respond with aggression, launching a counter-attack to hurt the one who wounded them. Hurling insults, planning a response that will really cut someone down, ruminating on imaginary arguments until you have the chance to explode on someone - these are the fighters.

Flighters are gone before you can register their arrival. Their anxiety spurs them to leave every party before it starts, to avoid crowds and opt for the safety of Netflix and phone scrolling alone on their couch rather than making social commitments.

Freezers are paralyzed by fear. They never know how to respond; they don't have words to explain what they're thinking and feeling. They will let people walk all over them because they're just not sure how to set a boundary.

Which one do you lean towards in relationships? There isn't a wrong answer, it's just useful to have a self-awareness of how we are built and what our go-to response is. Recognizing this is the first step on the path to changing it. Each one of the fight, flight or freeze responses is a form of self-preservation, a strategy for getting through life. These behaviours might be easier to recognize in other people rather than ourselves, and we might respond in different ways at different times.

When romantic rejection is prevalent in our lives, a pattern can develop where we somehow always end up in romantic relationships with the same kind of challenges, seeing the same kind of rejection over and over. The temptation is to try to choose a better partner, which yes, is often helpful. But true freedom comes when we learn to identify the patterns in our own thinking and behaviour, and do the difficult mental work of walking into wholeness ourselves.

Healthy romantic relationships are not perfect, but they are made of two teachable people. There will always be opportunities to grow together and improve your relationship, but when we take responsibility for our side of the yard, when we are humble and open to change, we have a great foundation for a partnership that will last. If however, we are full of fear because of past rejections and old wounds, we will sabotage every new relationship that we have. Being rejected romantically does not mean that you will always feel afraid, insecure or intimidated. With healing from past rejection wounds and renewing your mind with the help of the Holy Spirit, it is possible to get a fresh start and find wholeness.

All 3 types of rejection we have looked at—familial, social, and romantic—these are all types of rejection that happen in relationship. Being rejected by other people. They each have unique challenges and messages that are delivered, and that require time and effort to recover from. When we are rejected by other people, it is natural and common to feel victimized. We begin to see ourselves as targets and adopt beliefs that help us understand why we have been rejected. We strive to figure out what is "wrong" with us, and then try to hide it, correct it, or overcompensate for it.

We become sensitive to future rejection and partner with the fear of it. We find behaviours that will help prevent us from being hurt again, and a sort of snowball effect begins as these experiences stack on top of each other until we feel stuck and pinned down by this giant in our lives. Rejection becomes the context that we view every relationship through.

Self-Rejection

Self-rejection is less obvious and less understood, but just as or maybe even more important. A more familiar term for the kind of self-rejection I am referring to is shame. Shame is, even in the smallest quantity, a toxic feeling. We are all familiar with it—we can even feel it physically. A heat that rises up through your body, flushed cheeks and a rapid heartbeat. When you've done something wrong and someone else is about to find out you can feel shame swell up from within you.

There is a subtle difference between shame and conviction, and it's one we should be aware of. Conviction is what happens when you have the Holy Spirit living inside of you. When you sin, whether other people see it or not, the Holy Spirit will bring conviction through His love. Because you have done something wrong, it causes sorrow and leads to repentance.

But shame has a goal of keeping you in a negative place. It is an accuser, not inviting you to wholeness but condemning you to darkness. Shame pins the sin or behaviour on our identity, and tells us that what we did is who we are. Shame is fear in disguise, and it's a liar. When you make a mistake, mess up, or make a bad choice, it is not who you are. There is help, hope, and grace flowing from God to you through the Holy Spirit.

Shame isn't always truthful, meaning that it will bring accusations that are not accurate. They may feel true—when you believe that you are unworthy of love, you feel ashamed of it. You have evidence to explain why you should be ashamed of who you are, and accept that evidence as sufficient to pass judgement. When we judge ourselves, we convict pretty harshly.

Once we've decided that these beliefs about ourselves are true—once we've allowed shame to convict us, we reject ourselves. We are often much harsher judges of ourselves than we are of others. Our standards that we hold ourselves to can be impossible to reach while we have a lot more grace for the people around us. The way that we talk to ourselves, our inner thoughts, can be so harsh that we would never say them out loud to another human.

A lot of times, we start to reject ourselves after people we love and trust have rejected us. Because we respect them and look up to them, we can make the mistake of giving them so much power and influence that we accept their judgements even when it is against us. Sometimes all it takes is to look at a picture someone took of us and we pass harsh judgement and decide that person in the photo is not worthy of love. Why is it that I can feel good about how I look in a photo, post it online, and then a photo that was taken 2 minutes later that someone has tagged me in I look like an absolute troll? It's the same person in both photos, same day, same outfit, but I decide that one of those versions of me is loveable and the other one should be discarded and hidden.

We reject ourselves when we judge ourselves. And the only One worthy of the job of judge is God—when we take that responsibility on we are stepping into His territory. I'm a big fan of reading Scripture in context, so I would love to copy and paste all of 1st John here, but I will trust that you have read it or can read it if you'd like. It's a beautiful letter from my favourite apostle that talks about what it means to be a child of God, how to live in fellowship with others and accept your identity as God's beloved. Here's a brilliant piece of theology from John:

> *"By this we shall know that we are of the truth and reassure our heart before him; for whenever our heart condemns us, God is greater than our heart, and he knows everything. Beloved, if our heart does not condemn us, we have confidence before God; and whatever we ask we receive from him, because we keep his commandments and do what pleases him. And this is his commandment, that we believe in the name of his Son Jesus Christ and love one another, just as he has commanded us. Whoever keeps his commandments abides in God, and God in him. And by this we know that he abides in us, by the Spirit whom he has given us."*

> *1 John 3:19-24*

We see in this Scripture that we can be quick to condemn ourselves, even when God is not condemning us. I know that I don't want to be a harsher judge than Him. If the Lord votes to acquit, I don't want to be voting against Him. He knows more, He understands more, and He is much greater than my own heart.

And what a beautiful promise, that when we are not condemning ourselves, we are able to approach Him with confidence. It's our own self-judgement that keeps us distant from the Lord, that keeps us from approaching Him, from hearing Him, from being in fellowship with Him. John shows us here that God is not looking for perfection; He's not asking for us to live up to any standard—all He commands is that we believe in Jesus and love one another. That is when His Spirit abides in us and we have that deep fellowship and communion with our Father.

If you have rejected yourself, you likely find it hard to approach God. You might feel distant, you might feel like it's hard to pray or that your prayers not only go unanswered but that He doesn't even hear you. If it feels hard to connect with our loving God it might be because you have already rejected yourself, you have condemned your own heart when He has acquitted you.

There is an invitation for you to approach Him again, to have that intimate abiding relationship that deep down you really desire. You may have convinced yourself that you are doing okay, that you know God and are saved and that is good enough. But without deep abiding fellowship, without the intimacy of the Holy Spirit, you are missing something that is vital to life and growth.

If it feels hard to connect with our loving God it might be because you have already rejected yourself.

Accepting ourselves as we are is the opposite of rejection. Acceptance is the beginning of love, and love is unconditional. Even if you've made mistakes, even if others have rejected you, even if you have habits that need to change, you are fully loved right where you are. Here's another verse from 1 John 3, this time from the Passion Translation:

> *"Beloved children, our love can't be an abstract theory we only talk about, but a way of life demonstrated through our loving deeds."*
>
> *1 John 3:18*

Love is not an abstract theory. Even when it comes to loving ourselves, it cannot be an abstract theory. It must be demonstrated, must be acted on. We cannot say we love ourselves if our thoughts are constantly full of condemnation and rejection. We cannot control if other people will reject us, but we are responsible for whether we reject or accept ourselves. Once we learn to treat ourselves kindly, and to think the things that God thinks about us, it becomes really hard to partner with rejection. It becomes difficult to say anything negative about ourselves when we are aware of what God says about us.

When you are under the weight of rejection and all the things it brings with it, it is hard to imagine a version of yourself that is free and whole. It feels as if you will always be held back by this giant, that no matter how much love you receive you will always be weak in this area. But the truth is that walking into wholeness is not only a possibility, it is God's plan for your life. He has a roadmap for how to get you there, and it's what He envisions for your future.

If you truly desire freedom, there is a cost to it. You have to decide if you're willing to be uncomfortable for a little while—change always is uncomfortable. You have to decide if you really value relationships, because it will require you to be humble and teachable while you learn a new way of thinking. If you decide to dig in and make some changes, freedom is not only possible, it is your inheritance. You have a right to the freedom that you've only imagined for yourself and admired in others.

4

Roots & Fruit of Rejection

Most of us can recall an early rejection experience from a parent, I'm sure you have some as well. The reality is, parenting is hard, and there's no degree you can get to prepare for it. Even the most loving, patient, well-meaning parents make mistakes, and those mistakes can have a lasting effect on the child. If you're trying to parent perfectly, you will fail. The best we can hope for is to parent well, and to teach our kids how to allow Jesus to minister to them when they've been hurt. Modelling forgiveness, repentance and surrender to Christ is the best thing you can do as a parent.

When I was a teenager, I was working at McDonalds and was training to become a manager. They have quite a system for training people, one of the best and most reproducible systems in the world. I remember being overwhelmed at the number of binders and files that were available to us as resources for the many different problems and scenarios that can arise in a fast-food restaurant. It's near impossible to go through them all and be properly prepared for anything that could happen.

Just when I felt like I was drowning in paperwork, the person training me told me, "Amy, you don't need to have every answer memorized, but you do need to know where to find the answers". He was modelling a Kingdom principle for me—we can't prevent every wound for our kids, but we can teach them where to go to get it fixed.

If even the best parents cause rejection wounds, then there are many of us who will have to deal with incredibly painful memories of rejection. Parents who are not able to be there for their kids, parents who are still struggling with their own wounds, those who have physical or mental health challenges, or a myriad of other stressors and challenges - they can unintentionally create traumatic rejection wounds for their children. When this happens at a young age and we don't understand where to go to get it fixed, we find a way to make sense of it in our little brains and hearts.

Do you remember the first time you realized that not every family had the same weird traditions your family had? I remember the day I learned that not everybody knows what a Jordan's Special is. I thought it was everyone's favourite breakfast treat, a waffle (or two) topped with peanut butter and chocolate chips. It does sound quite unappealing now at my old age, but as a kid I thought it was the ultimate delicacy, and assumed I could walk into any friends house and request a Jordan's Special.

It turns out that was only "normal" in my home, where my brother (Jordan) invented it. When you're young, you assume that every experience you have is "normal", and so you create a belief system around your "normal" until someone presents another option. With rejection, if we experience it at a young age and are left on our own to process it, we create a belief system around it. Most often, that belief system is centred around rejection becoming our identity. We take the other persons action and interpret it as a comment on our identity. Our identity is how we define ourselves, the characteristics that we deem most important about ourselves. We run into trouble when we allow other people, or our own feelings to define our identities, rather than the God who created us.

When I was a kid, my house was a busy place. I'm the youngest of 4 kids, and my mom also ran a daycare out of our home. So in addition to the 4 of us, there were also 7-8 other kids running around at any given time. Some of my earliest memories are coming home from school and wanting to reconnect with my mom. School felt like such a scary place—there is so much independence that we ask from kids from a really young age.

Upon arriving home, I remember standing in the doorway, seeing the chaos of all those kids gathered together, and my mom would ask me how my day was. Before I could answer, someone would have a need, someone would spill a cup of milk, or someone else would walk in the door. I never got the chance to answer, and I interpreted this as rejection. As a 6-year-old, I learned that my voice didn't matter, that no one wanted to hear about my day, that I should stay quiet in the background and process everything internally.

Now as an adult, with varied experiences and a solid understanding of my identity in Christ, I can look back on those memories quite differently. I can see that my mom was doing the best she could with what she had, that she was not rejecting me but rather trying to provide for our family. I know now that there was no malicious intent behind what happened in my home, but even so, a wound was created. I'm sure that my mom was not looking at me and thinking "I have no desire to hear what Amy has to say; I wish she wasn't here," but that is the meaning I assigned to the message. It was the way my little brain made sense of the world around me, and many of us have similar stories.

It's actually a very self-centred worldview that interprets other people's actions as messages about you. Most of the time, other people's actions are in fact, about them. If you can relate at all to 6-year-old me, you will see how I started to define my identity by these rejection experiences. Kids are still forming their identities as they gain independence from their parents. This was my "normal," so I assumed that everyone felt the same way about me, that nobody would actually want to hear me speak. I built a belief system around my experience of my voice not having any value.

This example of coming home and feeling disconnected is just one memory I have of feeling rejection. There were many more that built upon this belief system and cemented my identity as "Rejected." I didn't know better, and that's okay. There's so much more grace available than we think! We're all doing the best we can with what we know, and when we look back at our younger selves, we need to extend grace to them too.

The enemy doesn't play fair, especially with children. If he can get a foothold in our thoughts when we are young, he will use that to open a door, and rejection and fear is one of the first and most common doors that he tries with children. In my home growing up, I had a lot of nightmares, night terrors, and experienced demonic spirits in our home at night. After everyone was asleep, I would be woken up by voices calling me, and they were not human.

You might brush this off as a kid having a nightmare or

imagining things, but it is actually quite common with people who have a prophetic calling on their life—as children, they have heightened experiences like this in the night. I remember many nights when I felt terrified and alone. My parents were asleep in the other room, but I felt completely abandoned. I didn't know what to do, but I knew I was scared and needed help.

Somehow, I had learned that the name of Jesus was powerful, and I would sit on the floor in front of my bed and repeat His name over and over until the terror faded. I desperately wanted Him to show up like the Jesus on the felt boards at Sunday School, where He entered the picture and completely changed everything. Instead there was something more important happening: a very real spiritual battle in the unseen realm. As a child, I was learning about spiritual warfare, and I was learning about the authority I carried as a Christian. I was alone physically, but even at that young age, the Holy Spirit inside of me was providing everything I needed.

I remember a little laminated card that stood on my dresser; every day of my childhood I would see it there at the beginning and end of my day. Those long nights when I was unknowingly being trained in spiritual warfare, I would see that card. It had my name, Amy, and under that the definition, which is of course, Beloved. Below that was a Bible verse...a Psalm I think, one talking about God's great love for me. I'm pretty sure this card was a gift from my grandma, sweet Marie. It was a great gift, completely well intentioned, but I grew to despise it.

It felt so completely contrary to my experience and what I knew to be true. I did not feel loved at all, much less Beloved, a much-loved person. I would stare at that word, Beloved, and feel like a fraud. I refused to accept that as my identity because it was contrary to my feelings. I had already accepted my identity as Rejected, and even kids instinctively know that a house divided cannot stand. Two different identities can't both be true. Either

I'm Beloved or Rejected, and I chose to partner with rejection. Rejection had come to define me and was what I understood best. I knew how to see it coming; I knew how it would feel, and I knew what I had to do to protect myself.

When we partner with rejection at a young age, a door is opened and the enemy then has legal spiritual authority to take all kinds of ground. Because other people are always involved in rejection, there is unforgiveness and bitterness that begin to grow. Any time you are holding on to unforgiveness you are partnering with the enemy—we'll take a closer look at this in Chapter 6. When we agree with something through our thoughts, we give it permission to grow. That's why Philippians 4:8 is such a key verse for spiritual warfare and for overcoming rejection.

> *"Finally brothers, whatever is true, whatever is honourable, whatever is just, whatever is pure, whatever is lovely, whatever is commendable, if there is any excellence, if there is anything worthy of praise, think about these things."*

Philippians 4:8

In the next verse, he states that if we think about these things, the God of peace will be with us. It stands to reason then, if our thoughts are focused on dishonour, injustice—things that are ugly, dark, wrong, and inferior—it will be hard to find peace. Negative thoughts tend to ferment—they bubble and grow and produce new features until it no longer resembles what you started with. We tend to give them permission to stay because they start small; things like sadness and anger aren't really harming anyone at the beginning, and you feel like you are still in control. But they are not passive forces—they are active and will grow until you are the one being controlled.

If you start with bitterness, left unchecked it can grow into anger, and anger left unchecked can grow into rage that destroys other people. If you start with sadness, left unchecked it can grow into depression and anxiety. Depression unchecked can grow into suicidal thoughts that will destroy your life.

If you have ever watched crime shows on TV, you've probably been appalled at the violence and the way seemingly average human beings can suddenly kill another person. You may have exclaimed to yourself in shock "I could never do that!" There's always an interview with some neighbour or friend of the guy, remarking that he seemed so normal, and how he always was helpful and kind. And he was, until the seeds of negative thoughts grew out of his control. The train is harder to stop the longer you let it chug down the track!

When someone experiences traumatic or long-term repeated rejection, the response can sometimes be to become emotionally numb. People will actually stop feeling anything because the feeling is too painful. Rejection leads to decreased empathy, and increased aggression. Many of the mass murderers over the last 30 years are people who experienced painful social rejection. They had become numb, had lost empathy and had become increasingly aggressive. While rejection is obviously not the only factor in shooting sprees, this information should be a big red flag to all of us that when rejection is allowed to go unchecked in our lives, this is the path it is leading us on.

This is the end goal of the enemy—steal, kill, destroy. He doesn't care whose life he is destroying; destruction itself is the goal. Rejection even temporarily lowers your IQ, short term memory, and decision making.

That's why when you have just been rejected, it's hard to think clearly, and it's wise to not make any major decisions in that delicate state. This also explains why so many of us get drastically bad haircuts after a painful breakup!

There has been more research being done in the last few decades on the relationship between our brains and our bodies and how there are physical ramifications to the things that we believe and foster in our thought lives. The book, *A More Excellent Way: Be in Health* by Dr. Henry W. Wright is a great resource if you want to learn more about the spiritual roots of physical disease.

I know in my own life, I have seen great breakthrough in my physical health after receiving healing for my spirit. I have been overweight most of my life, and definitely had addictions to junk food and was dependent on sugar. I was controlled by intense cravings for empty calories and felt like I was enslaved to it. I would also have cycles of intense commitment to health, where I would eat only rabbit food and exercise with intensity. I rarely saw any weight loss and was incredibly frustrated that no matter what I did I could not make any progress in my health.

It wasn't until I walked through incredible inner healing that I saw any physical change. The Lord was so kind to allow me to come to my rock bottom, a time when everything was stripped away and I was quite literally alone. My worst fears had come true, I had been completely rejected and had lost everything that I thought could bring me value. I was 30 years old, and I had lived my whole life with that self-label of Rejected on my forehead, expecting it everywhere I went. My worst fear was to be alone, and my worst fear had come true.

I started out life with some perceived rejection, which was left unchecked and grew into a monster that overshadowed every relationship and circumstance. It had multiplied from rejection into fear of rejection, bitterness, depression, anxiety, anger, pride, and so much more. And when that monster was finally standing over me, every worst fear realized, I wanted to die. I wanted to end my life because I had never imagined anything past that. It felt like the end had arrived, and I wanted to partner with that too. But just like in my childhood, when I was alone in my room, terrified and afraid, the Holy Spirit was with me. When I started to take action to end my life, He gently got my attention.

He showed me that I had reached the end of rejection, the ultimate betrayal and abandonment, and I was still there. I no longer had anything to fear because every fear that I had, had all come true. There was nothing left to ruminate on, nothing left to grow because I had faced my Goliath, and I was still standing.

I was in intense personal pain from the rejection, but there was nothing left to fear. It was the most incredibly freeing moment of my life. It's so hard to describe the complexity of that moment, the tension of deep wounds from people I really cared about, but also complete and immediate freedom from the fear of rejection. I also felt the incredible nearness of God in that moment. I felt the intimacy of understanding between Him and I, the excruciating rejection and betrayal that He faced at the end of His life mirrored in the rejection I was facing. They are not comparable, the rejection of Christ and my own, but we do ourselves a disservice when we try to compare emotional pain.

There is no universal measurement for pain. If you are wounded and go to the hospital, they will ask you to give your pain a number from 1-10. There is no test you take, no scale used, rather the doctor trusts the patient to evaluate and determine the severity of the pain. Trust is extended to each of us to determine our relative pain. A "5" on the pain scale might mean something different to me than it does to you, and that's okay.

With emotional pain, we need to be better at evaluating our own pain and trusting ourselves with that. Denying the pain does nothing to help you heal. Recognize the pain you are feeling, and even give it a number from 1-10. Recognizing where you are is the first step in determining how you move forward.

That day my pain was a 10 for sure. It might have been a 6 for you, if you don't have the same history and experiences and personality that I do. For me, it was a 10. When we compare our pain to others', we are hiding from the severity of it. If you tend to brush off your pain with statements like, "it could be worse," or stating that other people have experienced worse abuse, I would encourage you to pause and rate your own pain on an internal scale. Somebody else having a larger wound does not mean that your wounds don't hurt.

Denying the pain does nothing to help you heal.

Jesus experienced His own 10/10 pain, and even though our stories are different, our shared experience of the 10/10 rejection wound brought me closer to Him. I would love to tell you that Jesus appeared in my room right then, or I heard the audible voice of God, or an angel showed up with a magic drink that made me feel all better. The truth is much less exciting. I began the long slow work of healing, and I did it despite what I was feeling. I knew God was with me; my faith was strong enough to believe that He was there. But I didn't feel Him. I felt angry and humiliated and hurt. I took so much time over the next days and weeks just expressing the pain I was feeling. Journalling, crying, praying out loud. I processed it in detail, in different ways. Even painting my pain in watercolours was helpful.

If you did not grow up in an environment that allowed you to express pain, I highly encourage you to cultivate that skill now. It is not too late! Emotional granularity is the skill of identifying and giving a label to what you are feeling. Rather than just feeling "bad," "depressed," or "angry," taking the time to drill down and find a more specific label for what you are feeling can be really helpful. You know the feeling when someone else puts words to an experience you've had, through a song or poem? That's emotional granularity.

It's incredibly satisfying to be able to label things correctly and to give a name to what is going on internally for you. You can search online for an "emotion wheel"—this will show you a chart that has examples of more granular emotions, but know that the important part is expressing what you feel. Look for different ways to do this—art, music, conversation, physical activity—all are helpful.

Expressing pain is like expressing a wound—squeezing it until all the infection is drained out. We're actually born to be naturally good at this—if you've ever spent any amount of time with a baby, you know they are masters of expressing pain. Physical or emotional, their first instinct is to cry. Let it out. Express the wound. Have you ever met a baby with a grudge? No! They don't carry wounds with them; they process them in real time.

It's only when we, the all-knowing adults, teach them that expressing pain is only okay in some environments and conditions, that we teach them to hold on to wounds. And as we get older, we find that the places that are safe to express our pain get smaller and smaller.

Now I'm not saying we should all walk around wailing like babies at every perceived offense, but we could do a lot better at being aware of the pain we feel and creating space to express it. Some of us only ever process when we are with other people. There's nothing wrong with talking it out with someone you trust, but I highly recommend learning how to process your pain with the Lord before you process with people. I want to know what He thinks before I hear other opinions. If we really do value Him as our primary relationship, it should be reflected in the choices we make. If we always hear someone else's opinion first, it becomes harder to hear the Lord if He is saying something different. It is important to have people who are mature and trustworthy speak into our lives, but we need to be able to hear from God directly, and then consider their input.

When I was at my lowest point, I found myself completely alone, but by the grace of God I had just booked an appointment with a counsellor the week before. I knew I had some issues to work on, but God was really looking out for me because I at least had that session booked, and I knew I could hold on until then. I'm a big fan of Christian counselling and even medication when it is needed. I've done both. Everything you are doing to pursue healing needs to be in partnership with the Holy Spirit and to be in season. So often we don't know the season we're in, and we hold on to an old instruction from God, an old word, rather than hearing His word for today.

He exposed the roots of rejection in my life, and everything was brought into the light.

What I mean to say is, there is no formula for emotional healing. I can share my story; I can give you some tools, but you are a complex and unique individual and the only one brilliant enough to unravel all the pieces is the One who created you, who lives inside you, the Holy Spirit. Ask Him what your next step is in moving forward—what is the Next Right Thing.

If you're like me, you want a roadmap to wholeness with every possible option laid out. Jesus tends to be more of a story guy, inviting us to take another step and then decide together where to go. For me, counselling was the next right thing. But this wasn't just any counselling, it was a woman who took me into the Presence of Jesus and let Him minister to me. At home, I was expressing my pain and releasing all the emotion that I had been holding on to out of confusion for years.

I had been so focused on trying to do the proper thing, that I had denied any feeling that didn't agree with that. I was performance and perfection focused, thinking that I could stop people from rejecting me and control my environment. At counselling, Jesus was gently taking me back to some of my earliest memories and the places I had first started to fear rejection.

By going back to the start of the problem, God was breaking down those false ideas I had built about my identity. He exposed the roots of rejection in my life, and everything was brought into the light. He showed me how that little girl had opened the door to rejection by saying "Yes, Rejected is who I am," and the incredible compassion that He had for me.

Rejection is never God's plan for us, but He's also never afraid of it, even when He considers our humanity and weakness. To be honest, when I was upset, I wanted to see that Jesus was upset too. I wanted Him to grieve with me, to weep and to help me get revenge. But in that season, every time I looked at Him, He was smiling. Not in a condescending way, but in an inviting way. I was curiously frustrated. It made me take a step closer and ask Him why.

This would often happen in counselling sessions—I'd close my eyes and have a conversation with Jesus, relaying both sides of the conversation to my counsellor. She would occasionally guide me with a question to ask or a prompt. If this sounds odd to you, let me explain a few things.

The majority of communication is non-verbal. It's why emails and text messages are prone to misunderstanding, and if it's an important conversation you know that you need to have it in person. Watching a person's face, their gestures and movements, the tone in their voice—this all communicates part of the message to you. If you had a relationship with somebody that was only through written words, you would not be having a full experience or understanding of who that person is. If you have the Holy Spirit living inside of you, you are enjoying direct communication. He is always speaking and revealing Himself through the world around you.

We learn to hear God and how He speaks to us through the Holy Spirit. He can use our thoughts, our feelings, our dreams, other people, and of course, Scripture. However we hear God, we test what we heard against Scripture. If it doesn't agree with His Word, it wasn't Him. Prayer is meant to be a two-sided conversation—we are actually meant to hear God and respond to Him. In John 10, Jesus refers to us as sheep, and that we know our Shepherd's voice.

God also created our imaginations, and He will use our mind's eye to speak to us. Yes, our imagination can be influenced by evil spirits or our own desires, but they are not inherently evil. We are meant to do the work of valuing Scripture, knowing God's voice, and measuring the things we hear ourselves or through other people against that standard. Every time you hear someone preach or read a book, this one included, you are responsible to discern whether it aligns with the Shepherds voice. The same is true for our imaginations! You can engage with God in this way right now. Close your eyes; can you see in your mind's eye where Jesus is in the room right now? You can begin to interact with Him in this way, and allow Him to speak to you. Continue to submit these encounters to Scripture, and although they don't carry the same weight, they can be really valuable. This is the kind of encounter I was having with Jesus in that counselling room. I was full of pain, at the end of my rope, completely rejected. But when I approached Jesus, He was always smiling. It's as if He knew something I didn't.

5

Repentance

One of the most dangerous positions to be in is that of a victim. When there is a traumatic event, the victim doesn't just suffer once—often the worst part is the devastating effects that last long after the event has ended. In recent years there has been a push to refer to trauma victims as "survivors" rather than "victims". Both words are true, but one is more helpful. One positive, one negative, both acknowledging the reality of what they went through, but only the label of "survivor" allows the person to live from a place of victory.

A person who is labelled a victim will often find themselves living in that reality and finding it difficult to move forward. I remember at a young age, someone I trusted labelled me a martyr, I cannot remember what I said that had preceded it (aren't we so much better at remembering other peoples mistakes rather than our own?) I vividly remember a number of times as a young girl mockingly being called a martyr and I quickly learned to hide that part of me. After looking up what the word martyr meant, I knew it was not a compliment. From a young age, I had a victim mentality, a martyr complex, whatever you want to label it. I was hurting; I was learning to expect it everywhere I went, and I was also learning to hide it.

I wish at that point that I would have learned to see myself as a survivor; I wish that I had been able to forgive the people who were hurting me and hear what God was saying to me. I wish I knew then what I know now, and that's why I'm writing this book. Because I could have saved myself a lot of pain and a lot of years if I had a right understanding of what was happening in me and around me.

The problem that I had at the time, as a victim and a martyr, was that I saw other people's sin so much more clearly than I saw my own. I wasn't wrong, but it wasn't the full picture. It's the classic story that Jesus warns about in Matthew 7, where we ignore the stick in our own eye while pointing out the flaws in others. We do much better when we address our own sin and allow the Lord to deal with our brothers and sisters. When I say we do better, I really mean it.

These guidelines from the Lord are His kindness to us, not His punishment. He warns us about this kind of hypocrisy because He knows that it actually damages and holds us back, and that we will have more freedom and success when we are quicker to notice our own sin than we are to see others'. Any kind of sin is rebellion against the Lord, and the problem with rejection is it distracts us from the real problem. There are so many different angles the enemy works through rejection, and it looks different for each of us, but usually follows a pattern like this:

1. You are rejected (or perceive rejection)

2. Enemy accuses you of being (fill in the blank) that caused the rejection

3. Enemy encourages you to harbour bitterness, judgement and unforgiveness towards the person who rejected you

4. Enemy justifies step 3 and blinds you to your own sin

You'll see that in steps 1 and 2, you haven't done anything wrong. At this point you are an innocent victim, and are fighting both the pain of the wound and the pain of the accusation; whatever you believe the cause of the rejection is. For example, a woman who is dumped by her boyfriend might believe it's because she is unattractive. Whatever the actual reason was for him walking away, she is now fighting the pain of being dumped and a belief that she is unattractive.

Then she also has to deal with forgiving her ex. If at any point in those steps she partners with a lie, refuses to forgive, or makes judgements about him, she is rebelling against the Lord and that is now her #1 problem. However, the enemy will work to justify her own rebellion and to keep her focus on the first 3 things.

As a victim and a martyr, I saw other people's sin so much more clearly than I saw my own.

This happens all the time, and it happens to all of us. It is the reality of living in this broken world, on this side of Heaven, that when we are hurt by other people, we immediately are faced with a choice of either love or rebellion, even when we've done nothing wrong. There are opportunities every day for us to become victims, to partner with lies, to walk in bitterness, and to foster pride. If we label ourselves as victims, we will be blind to our own rebellion. That's why repentance is so important. Repentance does not mean that other people are innocent, and it does not mean that your wounds don't hurt. It is as simple and as painfully difficult as honestly acknowledging where you have turned away from the Lord.

My perspective totally changed when I began to see what Jesus saw. When I came to Him with my devastating rejection wounds, He gently began to show me my sin. He revealed that I was holding on to unforgiveness. Then He showed me that when I had not trusted Him, that I had built up defence systems to stop myself from being hurt again. And He showed me that I had pride, stemming from my desire to hide just how much I had been rejected.

Every time I came into His Presence, approaching Him with my open wounds, He would lovingly redirect my attention to the plank in my own eye. The biggest breakthrough I had was the day Jesus showed me His sadness. Remember how I told you every time I encountered Jesus He was smiling? He was never mad or worried, always peaceful. Well, at counselling one day, as I entered an encounter, Jesus didn't have His usually calm smile. He was sad. At first, I thought He might be sad for me—finally we would talk about the pain of my wounds! Not this day.

He began to show me what He saw; that for years, decades actually, I had been doing two things: I had not believed the words that He had spoken about me, and I had valued other people's opinions about me more than His. It was heartbreaking. I grieved deeply that day, grieved with this Jesus who ever-so-gently called me to repentance. I saw how His love had been offered but rejected by me. I was doing the very thing I hated and feared. I was rejecting Him every time I accepted negative thoughts about myself. I was rejecting Him when I allowed another person to have the power to destroy my self image.

The enemy doesn't play fair. This is how he operates: he has us partner with the very thing we despise in others. It is often the biggest sin in our lives that we are so quick to judge in others—the very thing that offends you is often the thing that is hiding in the background of your life. When these things are allowed to grow in our lives over time, we often find ourselves doing the very thing we hate to see others do.

They are hidden from our view until our hearts are ripe for repentance, until we have been opened to the love of God and have been touched by His kindness. Romans 2:4 says it's "the kindness of God that leads us to repentance," and that is my testimony to you as well. That day, for the first time, I clearly saw how I had been rejecting the Lord and others in my attempt to prevent being rejected myself.

I saw how His love had been offered but rejected by me. I was doing the very thing I hated and feared.

This was my greatest sin, and as soon as I saw it clearly, I despised it. One of the greatest prayers we can pray is for the Lord to help us to see our sin clearly. I repented immediately; repentance is, after all, just a turning of the heart. It is to choose a different path, and as soon as I saw what I had done, I turned from it. I grieved, and at the same time, I received the forgiveness of the One I had rejected.

There is no waiting period for forgiveness, just an ever-increasing awareness of how forgiven we really are. There was a marked change in my life from that day forward, and I will never forget that moment. I want to live my life from this conviction, to always be more aware of my own sin than of others'. To be more critical of my own motives than of those around me. To be quicker to repent than to convict. Perhaps ironically, I don't know if I've ever felt more loved than I did that day. True repentance does that, it restores the standard of love and intimacy between you and the Lord. It is not a process of feeling convicted, apologizing and then acting differently. Repentance is an immersion in the love of God itself.

We tend to think that the different aspects of God's character are separate from each other—that sometimes He is loving, and sometimes He is wrathful. We want to be close to the New Testament version and distant from the Old Testament version of God. We want to catch Him in a good mood, when He's the Jesus holding children on His lap and shouting "Blessed are the poor!", and we want to head out for a walk when Jesus is flipping tables and tearing down Pharisees. I believe we are attempting an impossible task when we try to compartmentalize God in this way. God IS love, and therefore He is never without it. His discipline is His love. Even His wrath is His love.

That is why, in a moment of true repentance, you should feel the love of God. False repentance is what happens when we try to change our behaviour without being open to the love of God, which remember, includes the discipline of God. We feel bad about the thing we are doing, the habit of sin that we can't seem to break, and so we try to fix it. We think we are repenting when we feel bad about ourselves and try to stop doing the thing. But true repentance is when we allow God's love to break us open, and get close enough to Him to see the real sin in our lives, to see where and how we have rebelled against Him. All too often, we are so focused on behaviour that we are blind to the deeper problem, the root of rebellion. I have seen in my life that I am powerless to change without the love of God, and the more access I give Him, the more freedom I get.

Another thing we need to watch out for with rejection is pride. It sounds counter intuitive, because most often when we are feeling rejected, we have a low self-esteem. Pride feels like the furthest thing away when you are lonely, rejected, and depressed. So many negative thoughts about how nobody values you, appreciates you, or wants to be around you. You are thinking so lowly of yourself, how can you possibly be called prideful? When you are engaging in false humility, you believe you're being humble, that you are honouring other people and doing the right thing. Any time you believe you know better, that no one else can speak into an area of your life, it should be a red flag for pride. This is actually a twisted expression of pride known as false humility. It's another way the enemy deceives us and distracts us from what is really going on in our hearts.

When we think of pride, often what we are actually thinking of is conceit. Conceit is an excessively favourable opinion of oneself. This is the classic image of pride, a smug classmate who takes all the credit for a project he didn't help with. A better word for pride might be superiority—an excessively high opinion of one's position. Believing that your way of doing things is better, that your feelings are more important, that everyone should adjust to you. This is pride, and this is where false humility hides. False humility makes negative statements about you, while refusing to accept any positive statements, whether that is from other people or the Lord. It is holding your opinion as the highest, even when that opinion is negative.

False humility is especially damaging because it packs a 1-2 punch. It is first demeaning oneself, refusing compliments and reinforcing negative self talk, and then it is also elevating yourself above others. For example, when you refuse a compliment you are first saying "No, I'm not that good/nice/talented/beautiful,"… and at the same time you are saying "My opinion is more important than yours." These false humility statements are half-truths that are really difficult to argue with, because you have built an identity around these things. You have probably been making these kind of statements about yourself for a long time, mostly inwardly. When we do this with other people, we are putting ourselves above them, and when we do this with the Lord, we are putting Him below us. And that is incredibly prideful. It's the same thing that Satan himself did, he started to think that he should be above God, and that is rebellion.

True humility is when you are confident of your identity and value, without concerning yourself with your position. Both sides of pride are about positioning—either higher than others (pride), or lower than others, while holding your opinion as higher (false humility). True humility is not at all about your position: it's not about seeing yourself as lower than others. True humility is no longer being concerned with your position at all. It is knowing who you are and being willing to love and serve whoever is in front of you because position is not on your radar. The day you realize that your identity is not tied to your position is the day you are living in true humility.

Jesus Christ is of course, the picture of true humility. Confident in His identity, in God's identity, and unconcerned with position. Knowing that He was God incarnate and yet being willing to come as a baby in a manger, willing to die for sinners, and willing to wash the feet of the friends who He knew would betray Him. That is true humility. There are no Scriptures of Jesus demeaning Himself—you won't find a verse of Him arguing "No, really, I'm not that nice!". We never see Christ overcompensating with false humility when the devil tempts Him with pride. When Jesus is in the wilderness, the first thing the enemy does is to invite Him to turn stones into bread. Which He could do, and was able to do, but it was not what God was doing in that moment.

Whereas I, in my false humility, would have denied my authority in that moment, and a prideful person would have jumped at the opportunity to prove his abilities and turned those stones into bread so he could try to hold on to his position. Jesus, in true humility, knew He did not prove His authority to keep His position. And He did not need to justify or make an excuse for why He wouldn't do it in that moment. He had nothing to prove and nothing to justify. He knew that His identity was not tied to His position or His performance.

One of the most dangerous things we can do is to soften sin. Giving sin a name that allows it to stay is giving it permission to grow. For example, when I was in the depths of that rejection pain and wounds, I thought my false humility was just humility. I thought that when I was making myself small and low that it was the right thing to do. It was only when I allowed the Holy Spirit to show me what it really was that I had the power to make changes in my life.

Another sin that we often soften is people pleasing. When we give so much power to people that we put them above the Lord, we are rebelling against God. It often feels like we are just trying to be kind; you may call it being a good friend or being flexible or serving others. And it often does start that way. But when we start to prioritize or position other people in a place above the authority of God in our lives, we are people pleasing and we need to bring correction to that habit.

Anytime someone or something has the power to throw off our sense of security, we have something that needs to be adjusted. That is not to say that we don't feel disappointment or that we are not affected by the world and people around us. If we are in community and living on this earth for any amount of time, we will feel the effects of it. The point is that our hearts need to be soft enough to the conviction of the Holy Spirit that we can recognize when we start to cross the line from hurt to rebellion.

It's important that we have a lot of grace for ourselves and for each other. The goal here is not perfection but it is to soften our hearts. Over time, sin hardens us and makes us blind to the traps we are caught in, and it is the gentle whispers of the Holy Spirit that we want to be attentive to. None of us do this perfectly, and we should not expect perfection from each other.

If anyone has the right to require perfection, it is Jesus who lived perfectly Himself, and yet He has so much grace for us while we process and grow. Who am I to demand more than Christ Himself? If you tend to have more grace for other people than you do for yourself, make an adjustment. And vice versa; if you have a lot of grace for yourself but are quick to point out imperfections in others, make an adjustment. Grace is a universal standard; it has no measurement or requirements because Jesus Christ fulfilled the requirements for us.

I still am in the process of growing and becoming more secure when it comes to rejection and all the ways I tend to react to it. I still sometimes feel thrown off when I come across people who actually do reject me or who just say really insensitive things that feel like rejection. I'm learning how to slow down my reaction, be fully aware of my thoughts, and be intentional with my choices in those moments. I don't do it perfectly, but I have come a long way. I am living in victory over rejection, and I am seeing so much progress the longer I practice these things.

One of the things I really try to be aware of is the ways I tend to try to protect myself. We all have defaults based on our personalities, our past wounds and our fears. There are many ways we protect ourselves, and it can look different in different seasons of our lives. It can be putting up walls to not let people in, rejecting people before they can reject you, or trying to hold on tight to people so they don't get away. It can be intense criticism of the people closest to you, or becoming emotionally distant from everyone in your life.

Whatever you lean toward when it comes to protecting yourself from rejection, it unfortunately has the opposite effect of what you hope for. You end up creating distance between you and the people you love, which is the same outcome as rejection. When you're in the thick of it, you can even be aware that this is happening, but willing to continue because it feels like the only option, the lesser of two evils. At least you know what is coming and have a bit of control over the situation, rather than being completely out of control when others reject you.

Changing this pattern is only possible when we take responsibility for our part. Self-protection isn't itself evil, but it quickly leads us into rebellion if we're not careful. Again, this is a natural reaction to being wounded, and we need to have a lot of grace for ourselves, while also being sensitive to what the Holy Spirit wants to reveal.

The problem with any kind of self-protection is that it often does not factor in God Himself. We give other people so much power and none to the Lord. We of course can't actually remove God from power, but when we think about Him as powerless to help us, we have already made a choice to not give Him access to our lives and hearts. If we choose to take control to prevent further wounds, we are choosing to act independently.

A lot of us in today's Western culture have been taught that dependance is a negative thing and we need to stand alone and meet our own needs. We have learned to find solutions for problems with all the advanced technology and all the opportunities that it brings. We are an individualistic culture as opposed to the community based culture of ancient Israel and even still today in other parts of the world. When we have a world view that is individualistic, we see ourselves as self-dependant and disconnected. We learn to get our needs met in creative ways that don't require anything from other people.

This kind of mindset and worldview also begins to apply to our relationship with the Lord, and we see ourselves as independent and disconnected from Him. As a small example, I hear people talk about their finances in terms of either earning money themselves, or depending on the Lord. And I know what they're saying: that they are choosing either to work at a job and earn a paycheque, or to not work and rely on gifts and miracles to pay their bills. The problem is that it's an illusion to believe that we can control our own finances and earn money separate from God's provision. He provides for us, whether that is through a job or through gifts. They are different avenues from the same source.

Believing that some aspects of our lives are completely separate from God, that we can create or experience any good thing on our own merit is an illusion. Every good and perfect gift comes from our Father (James 1:17), and that includes the very breath in our lungs.

When it comes to our relationships with other people and our emotional health, we should be aware that we are never separate from God even in this area. He never leaves us or abandons us, and there is nothing that can separate us from His love.

> *"For I am convinced that neither death nor life, neither*
> *angels nor demons, neither the present nor the*
> *future, nor any powers, neither height nor depth, nor*
> *anything else in all creation, will be able to separate us*
> *from the love of God that is in Christ Jesus our Lord."*
>
> *Romans 8:38-39 NIV*

Think about that for a moment—anything else in all creation—this includes the people who have rejected you. When someone rejects you, even if everyone in the world were to reject you, you would still be perfectly held in the love of God, completely safe and connected to Him. It might not feel that way, but feelings are not evidence of truth they are indicators of our circumstances.

An awareness of this constant connection with the love of God is key to recovering well from rejection. When we remember that we are safe and connected to a loving God, we don't need to create ways to protect ourselves from pain. It doesn't mean that we will never feel pain, but it does mean that we know and trust that the love of God is really great at helping us heal, and that He is our ultimate Protector.

These self-protection strategies, be it controlling others, attacking others, or pushing people away, are strategies that help you emotionally survive a difficult moment. But when habits are created, we start to use these strategies when we are not in moments of crises. We start to use them in peaceful moments when we don't need protection, like a soldier carrying loaded weapons during peace time among civilians. We end up creating a lot of damage in the name of protecting ourselves, all based on an underlying fear that we are alone and disconnected from the love of God.

Before we can make much progress in renewing our minds, we need to first take an honest look at the ways we have been rebelling against the Lord, through self-protection, pride, and unforgiveness. We need to let our hearts be softened by the love of God so that we can repent and be restored to the healthy ways of relating to others, the freedom that Christ has provided for us. Repentance is serious business, but it is the safest, most free, and most loving place to be.

6

Forgiveness

In 1994, during the Rwandan genocide 800,000 people were murdered by their neighbours. The Tutsi people were demonized by the Hutus, with religion convincing them they needed to go to war to get rid of them. It was a brutal attack that also drove 2 million refugees out of the country. What started as a political and military attack, led to civilians taking up arms. This is when Hutu people who had been living somewhat peacefully next door to Tutsi people for a long time, invaded the homes of their neighbours and often used machetes to brutally murder innocent men, women and children. After 100 days of terror, the attacks were stopped.

As the country began to heal after the genocide, there were over a million court cases as people tried to find justice. I was able to travel to Uganda with YWAM in 2019, and got to meet many amazing people. Uganda sits on the northern border of Rwanda, and is not far from Kigali, the capital in Rwanda where the genocide began. The people there are still scarred by this terrorism, 25 years later still trying to recover. I also had the privilege of visiting a refugee camp on the northern border, where Uganda meets South Sudan.

For a week we stayed in their camp, a couple of friends and I. We shared meals of beans and posho—a local favourite that I could never quite grow to love. Posho is a maize flour that is boiled into a glue like consistency. It sticks to your ribs quite profoundly, so is welcomed by people who know what it's like to go hungry. There were beautiful mothers, small children, and some men as well. We played, we danced, and we worshipped the Lord together.

I was there to preach, to share some encouragement with these refugees, who had fled a brutal war and seen horrible atrocities. It was unlike any other room I have been in for a church service. It was a school room, and it also doubled as our guest housing. Bare concrete floors and walls, with large openings for windows. People were packed in shoulder to shoulder, and we were barely protected from a sudden storm and downpour of rain. The noise on the tin roof was so loud that I couldn't preach.

We worshipped instead, some of the refugees leading us in joyous songs and a djembe being passed around for different people to provide a beat. It must've been an hour or two until the storm passed, and we were able to settle in and hear each other again.

What I remember about that day is what I saw when I looked out over the crowd. I believe there were about 100 or so with us, and as I scanned their faces, I saw sorrow like I have never seen before. Yes, we had just been jumping and clapping in worship, but as the room settled, the grief that is always simmering just below the surface for these refugees bubbled up.

I could see in their eyes the trauma that they had lived through. They had seen their loved ones murdered in front of them. They had been abused and raped and barely escaped themselves, fleeing on foot with nothing but their lives and the clothes on their bodies. These people had lost not only their families, but had lost their innocence, their stability, and their peace as well.

At that point, it had been 25 years since the Rwandan genocide, and people had been making significant process as they tried to pick up the pieces of their lives. With help from different agencies, there were programs and aid made available to the surviving victims. There was an article in the New York Times a few years ago about reconciliation that was happening between the Tutsi and Hutu people. They had a series of pictures of survivors standing next to their attackers. Each picture also had a quote from each person, the attacker stating their regret and the victim sharing about their decision to forgive.

The women are standing beside men who invaded their homes and caused incredible trauma. Men who killed their children in front of them. What was incredibly moving to see is that these women describe the difference of a before and after. Not before and after the attack, but before and after the forgiveness. They describe how they were stuck in hatred and bitterness, until they made a decision to forgive, and after that, they felt freedom and peace return to them.

It's incredible to hear these stories of radical forgiveness because it shows us what is possible, what is available to us in our own lives. Forgiveness is not an abstract feeling that comes and goes; it is a decision that we have the privilege of making. It's not easy, and it doesn't solve every problem, but as we see with the brave Tutsi women, it is possible.

If forgiveness was an emotion, it would be easy. We would

do it when we felt like it, and when we didn't feel like it we would wait. But that's not a Kingdom view of forgiveness, it's a world view that doesn't match up with what we know as Truth. When Jesus talks about forgiveness He doesn't say "Wait until you feel like it," He just tells us to forgive people who hurt us. He knew it would happen; He didn't say "If your brother sins against you," He said "When." He knew it was going to happen and He told us what we should do in advance.

In Matthew 18, Jesus answers a question from inquisitive Peter about forgiveness. Peter asks him how many times he should forgive, maybe 7? 7 already represents completeness, so Peter probably felt pretty generous making that suggestion. Jesus ups the ante by responding with 77 times. If 7 represents completeness, 77 is a symbol of beyond complete—abundance. Jesus is saying that whenever you think you've reached the end of forgiveness, you're not there yet. He's saying keep going, keep forgiving. What's interesting is that way back in Genesis, we see a foreshadowing of this exchange. In Genesis 4, Lamech shares a poem known as the "Song of the Sword":

"Adah and Zillah, hear my voice;
you wives of Lamech, listen to what I say:
I have killed a man for wounding me,
a young man for striking me.
If Cain's revenge is sevenfold,
then Lamech's is seventy-sevenfold."

Genesis 4:23-24

Lamech is a descendant of Cain, the first man to murder another. Cain was unable to forgive his brother, and Lamech struggles with this as well. In his poem he vows that his revenge will be 77-fold. He's made a powerful declaration, one that many people hold today, that revenge is the solution.

Lamech's name even means "powerful," showing us just how important it is for us to choose between revenge and forgiveness. It is a powerful thing to seek revenge, and it is a powerful act to extend forgiveness.

I love the redemption of Christ, that even this small detail didn't escape Him. He was there at the beginning and remembers how revenge first entered our world. He redeems every broken part of humanity—where the world says revenge seventy-seven times over, Jesus says forgive seventy-sevenfold.

The choice we have around forgiveness is not "Do I feel like forgiving?" but it is "Do I want revenge, or forgiveness?" Saying no to forgiveness is saying yes to revenge. There is no middle ground, there's no "Well I don't forgive him, but I don't want to see him hurt." We tend to soften these things by trying to stay in a gray area, trying to coddle our feelings without having to take a decisive action. But when it comes to forgiveness, inaction is action. Not choosing to forgive is choosing to not forgive.

The world tells us that forgiveness is given out based on the feeling of the one who was hurt, or that it depends on the apology of the one who caused the hurt or their ability to "make it up" to them. The world sees forgiveness as something that you earn, with enough reparations and promises to not do it again. The balances need to be evened out, their needs to be a payment made to make things right. But if you are a Christian, if you believe the gospel of Christ and the good news of the Holy Bible, it has to change the way we think about things like forgiveness. We should look different than the world does.

So what is forgiveness exactly? It is, at its simplest definition, giving up the power to punish. Allowing someone to be released from a debt or a sentence. We tend to naturally use the word "unforgiveness" to describe the opposite, but unforgiveness is not actually a word. You can't find it in a dictionary. We already have a word for what the opposite of forgiveness is; it's called revenge. Revenge requires payment or punishment for wrongdoing. Again, words like unforgiveness or bitterness soften the sin that hides behind them. The sin that we partner with when we refuse to forgive is actually a pretty serious one, and it's a sin against Christ Himself.

When Christ died on the cross, He didn't just take on the sins of one person. He died for you, yes, but not just for you. He died for the sins of the world. His blood paid for it all. It's the very foundation of our faith, Jesus died on the cross and saved us from sin and death and hell.

> *"My little children, I am writing these things to you so that you may not sin. But if anyone does sin, we have an advocate with the Father, Jesus Christ the righteous. He is the propitiation for our sins, and not for ours only but also for the sins of the whole world."*

> *1 John 2:1-2*

We love the cross for our own salvation, but we despise it for the ones who have hurt us. It is a harsh reality to face, that when we choose revenge over forgiveness, we are saying that the blood of Christ is not enough. The cross is not enough, we want more payment. That is the truth of the choice you are making when you choose not to forgive. It is an ugly thing to face. Either the blood atones, or it does not.

If that is the choice you want to make, to say that the blood atones for you but not your neighbour, you are free to make it. You are free to demand more payment, more punishment. But be aware of your choices, don't hide them or soften them. This is what Jesus was talking about when He shared the parable in Matthew 18 of the unforgiving servant.

The servant who owed a debt of 10,000 asked the king for forgiveness. He was granted it and gratefully received that forgiveness, and then turned around and immediately demanded he be paid back the 100 that he was owed from a fellow servant. He was unwilling to extend the same grace that he received.

In Matthew 18:32 the Lord calls this wickedness. He wants us to see how serious it is to reject the crucifixion of Jesus as payment for the sins that have been committed against us, while we claim it as sufficient for our own sin. If you accept Christ as your Saviour, you must accept His sacrifice as payment for the sins of your enemy as well. It is not a partial atonement, it is full.

We love the cross for our own salvation, but we despise it for the ones who have hurt us.

Years ago, I had a revelation from the Lord where He showed me what a privilege forgiveness is. I was struggling to forgive a friend who had rejected me. She had made promises and then changed her mind. Because I had been so stuck in the fear of rejection, I had made her work pretty hard to earn my trust over the years. I had a few hoops for her to jump through, and she did, but even then she let me down. I'm not saying I was in the right, but I was hurt. Her broken promises and disinterest in our friendship was really hurtful. After doing everything I could to prevent rejection, it happened again.

In my wounding I ran to Jesus, He had become my safest place. I was learning how to hear Him and give Him access to every part of me. As I met with Him that day, we were talking face to face. I could see that friend over His shoulder, and could feel all the pain of that rejection. Just seeing her made me feel all twisted up and yucky inside. I didn't want to forgive her. I didn't feel like forgiving her. I had talked to her about how much it hurt, and she didn't seem to care. There was no apology, no assurance she would try to not do it again. I didn't want to give her another chance to hurt me, so I was holding on to bitterness and revenge. I wanted her to change before I would forgive—that was the payment I required. I wanted her to be sorry and to change her behaviour. I was the servant demanding she pay back the 100 when I had already been forgiven 10,000.

Jesus took me gently by the shoulders, and turned me around so that I was looking the same direction He was. And when I turned, I saw my friend there as well. But I saw her as if I had already forgiven her. It was a sudden change, without making the choice yet He allowed me to see that when I choose to forgive, I get to see that person and not feel yucky. I can feel love and peace and safety. I knew instantly that I could love her and not require anything else. In forgiveness, I could release her and make choices moving forward about how much I wanted to have her in my life. I did not need anything from her.

The difference was not in anything she did, the difference was inside of me. And in that same moment, I saw how Jesus saw me the same way. He looks at me and does not see my sin or my mistakes. He feels nothing but love and requires nothing from me. I immediately understood what a privilege it is to forgive others the way He has forgiven me. It was a true revelation that I cannot fully communicate with words, and it has changed my life permanently. That was probably 7 or 8 years ago, and I have not struggled with forgiveness since then.

I've had people hurt me pretty deeply; I've had more rejections and malicious attacks. I've had people who were supposed to be safe and trustworthy betray me. It's been painful, but since having that revelation from Jesus I forgive immediately. My best advice about forgiveness is for you to pray for a revelation of your own sin. Ask God to reveal to you how much you have been forgiven, and forgiving others will become easy. Forgiveness is a privilege. We get to be like our heavenly Father, and we get to practice what He has modelled so well for us. Forgiveness feels like getting to go to work with your Dad as a kid—feeling grown up and important because you're acting just like Him. You get dressed up and pack a lunch and get to enter His world and see what He does all day. It's a privilege, an honour, an opportunity to mature beyond our current level.

"For if we have been united with him in a death like his, we shall certainly be united with him in a resurrection like his."

Romans 6:5

It's what this verse means, that being united with Christ is not just about the resurrection and the great benefits we personally get, it's also about dying to ourselves and being united in all ways. It is surrendering our own will for the will of our Father. And we find when we do this that dying is also to our own benefit. Just as the Tutsi women described, after choosing forgiveness they actually felt more free, more peaceful. It was good for them, even though it came at a cost.

Another thing that has been profound for me is to learn to walk through forgiving someone in a private process. We can be really quick to hash things out, to voice our hurt and make sure the other person knows what they've done. Especially if it's someone you see regularly or live with, we often need to address problems quickly so that they don't grow into something bigger. That's good of course, but if you need to work through forgiveness, I highly recommend doing that work with the Lord before you meet with the person who hurt you.

The point of having a conversation with someone who has hurt you is not to come to forgiveness; it is to come to reconciliation. Forgiveness only takes one person, but reconciliation takes two.

It is absolutely possible, and from my own experience I would say preferable, to forgive someone without ever hearing an apology. Without having any promises for change. Just as forgiveness does not require payment, it also does not require apologies. Forgiveness is when you release that person in your own heart and tell the Lord that you do not require payment or punishment for what they did. It is primarily about you and the Lord, secondarily about that person. This is why forgiveness is possible even if someone has died or is no longer in your life. It is a lie keeping you in bondage that says if they're not in front of you checking certain boxes, you cannot forgive them.

I have done it both ways—hashing it out with that person and hearing them apologize and make promises, and I have forgiven alone with the Lord before even talking to the person about what happened. I can tell you that the second way is much better for my spirit and soul.

When I was able to come into the conversation having already forgiven them, I was able to talk to them with honesty and vulnerability about what happened and how I was hurt, but only with the goal of connection, not of punishment. Because reconciliation was my goal in the conversation, I could communicate clearly, voice my concerns and speak with love the entire time. Those conversations were much more successful than the old ones, where I had a list of things I needed the other person to do and say in order to move forward.

When you process the pain of rejection and other wounds with the Lord before you take them to other people, you are setting yourself up for success. You get to be fully honest and vulnerable with Him, hearing what He has to say about it all, before going and approaching that person with humility, love and peace. It is possible to work through forgiveness in real time with the person who has hurt you, but you miss an opportunity for intimacy with the Lord. He's the best at helping us through those moments, and He always knows the right thing to say. He is the safest place to be.

I remember once I was with some friends at a campground, and some of the kids had a fight. One girl was hurt, and she was clearly mad at her friend. She came and sat near me and through tears told me what happened. I said something to her about how she probably needs to forgive her friend for what she'd done, and asked if she knew how to do that. Her reply showed the beautiful authenticity of children. She said "Forgiveness? No, I usually try either ignoring it or getting revenge." Brilliant honesty. "Hmm" I said, "how has that been working for you?"

If we could all be so honest to admit our own process. What do we choose when we are rejected or hurt? Ignoring it, getting revenge, or forgiving—the choices for a 10-year-old are the same as the choices for us as adults.

Forgiveness only takes one person, but reconciliation takes two.

A lot of people who struggle with forgiveness can't wrap their head around the permanency of it. You think you forgive someone, but then you're reminded of the hurt and you're back at square one. It's frustrating to feel like you have to flip flop every day with the emotion of it. In my experience this happens when we hold on to our right to revenge, but we're tired of feeling the effects of bitterness, anger, and hatred that come with it. We allow the feeling of forgiveness to come and go, without making a definite choice.

When there are large and deep wounds like this, we need the help of the Father. We need God's love to cover our wounds and begin to heal them. It's okay if this takes time. He is a gentle, loving Father that knows exactly what we need to walk into freedom, and He is faithful to help us through.

True forgiveness will take us past just being okay, to actually having love for the people who hurt us. Jesus teaches us to love our enemies. This is uncomfortable to talk about, but we can't just skip over the parts of the Bible that we don't like. Love is not neutral, merely tolerating and allowing someone else to exist. Love doesn't just stop being negative, it moves actively into the positive.

Anyone can love someone who is nice to them, but as Christians we are also called to love our enemies, and love requires forgiveness. It does not mean that the pain didn't happen, and it does not mean that you give that person freedom in your life. When the person you are forgiving and loving is not a safe person to be around, this is more about heart posture than action. Be aware of the different postures in your own heart of bitterness, neutrality, and love.

Often those relationships where you have been rejected or hurt by someone require new boundaries that have not been there before. But forgiveness does release them from all payment and punishment, and restores a posture of love. The only source we have for that kind of love is the God who created us, died for us, and has prepared a place for us in Heaven. With His help, we can be as free as the Tutsi women standing next to the Hutu men.

When you make a decision to forgive someone, feelings can still come and go. It doesn't have to scare us so much when we have feelings that are different from our thoughts and choices. You can be aware of it, recognize that there is still pain, that you're in a process of healing, but making a decision to forgive doesn't change when you feel another wave of pain from the loss, the hurt, or the sorrow. They are separate from each other even though they seem so closely tied. Your feelings will follow your thoughts, so when you choose to forgive someone, your emotions will catch up as long as you're allowing the Lord to heal your wounds as well.

In order to have that intimacy with the Lord, we need to address any bitterness we are holding towards Him as well. Remember anytime there is perceived rejection or hurt we need to deal with it and not hide from it. You might know logically that God does not sin and He has not tried to hurt you, but you might feel hurt. You might feel like He abandoned you, that He wasn't there for you when you needed Him, or that He didn't stop bad things from happening to you. You might be angry at God. Ignoring those feelings doesn't help, and getting revenge on God is a fruitless endeavour. Hiding from Him or withholding intimacy with God will only bring damage to your life.

Bring those emotions in all their honesty before the Lord, just like the Psalmists did. Follow the thoughts out and find the root. There is a lie at the root of these hurts—it might be that you believe God was not there for you. You might think that He doesn't love you, or that He is not trustworthy.

Anything that you have believed about God that does not line up with Scripture requires repentance. Repent before the Lord, receive His forgiveness, and ask Him to show you the truth. Allow Him to reveal where He was in those moments of hurt in your past, and allow Him to show you His heart for you in your darkest moments. Make a decision to believe it, whether it feels true or not.

We can cause pain for ourselves or others, sometimes intentionally and sometimes innocently. When we regret mistakes that we've made, we wish that we had handled something differently. It's tempting to hold on to those regrets and find ways to punish ourselves, deciding that we're not worthy of enjoying life, or that we should pay in little ways every day for mistakes we've made. It is time to let go, Beloved. Shame and regret are not noble or helpful, they are rebellion against God. You are denying the blood of Jesus and His forgiveness for you. He already paid for it; it is finished. Accept His forgiveness for every mistake in your past, and repent for believing the lie that your sin is stronger than His grace.

I encourage you to take some time before moving on to the next chapter, and invite the Holy Spirit to search your heart. Is there anyone else in your life that you need to forgive? Is there anyone who could walk into that room where you are right now, that would make your insides twist and turn? If there is any person that could walk through that door and make you feel yucky just at the sight of them, you have a choice of forgiveness or revenge set before you today. Picture your Saviour on the cross, thank Him for His sacrifice, and allow that to be enough. Grant the same freedom that you have received to the ones who have hurt you.

Father God, I thank you for the power of forgiveness. Thank you for the sacrifice of Jesus on the cross, that His blood atones for all sin and sickness. I choose this day to forgive (name those who have hurt you) for (name what you are forgiving them for). I release them from all payment and punishment, and set them free today. I bless (name) today in the name of Jesus and ask that You would bring the fullness of Your grace in their lives. Amen.

7

Renewing Your Mind

A renewed mind is something we are familiar with in Christianity, but most people in church couldn't tell you how to do it or what actually changes when your mind is renewed. There are a number of Bible verses we can find that talk about having a renewed mind, and it's something we all would like to have. A mind that doesn't give you any trouble, and only thinks good thoughts? Sign me up! The truth is, it takes time and effort to partner with the Lord in renewing your mind. But it is possible. With the help of the Holy Spirit and an understanding of how our brains work, we can make significant changes in our thought life.

There are four things required to renew your mind, and the good news is all of them are in your control. We'll take a look at them here, and then I will share some of the specific strategies that have helped me walk in victory over rejection. Hopefully you've been walking through the first few chapters, and have taken some time with repentance and forgiveness. You are well positioned to begin the more fun work of renewing your mind!

Humility

Humility and teachability go hand in hand. Teachability is one of the traits in other people that I find incredibly attractive. It is actually number 2 on my list for what to look for in a future husband. Number 1 is a love for Jesus, obviously. I remember I had a friend growing up who was so teachable she was always asking questions and being, what I thought was, embarrassingly honesty when she didn't know what something was. I would cringe, thinking she was about to be humiliated, that she couldn't just "play it cool" and act as if she knew what was going on. Being a teenager is tough, isn't it? She somehow came off as even more cool, when she disarmed people with her curiosity and teachability.

I was on the other end of the spectrum, I had learned some bad habits growing up and one of them was to nod and smile, and figure it out later. "Fake it till you make it" is what I lived by... and when that is functioning in a healthy way it helps me to figure out how to make things work, and how to learn new tasks. It forces me to dive in and be resourceful. It can be a great asset for sure. But in unhealthy seasons, that attitude has made me too proud to ask for help. It's distanced me from people who wanted to work together, and it can hold me back from making any progress.

When we are teachable, it means that we're willing to adjust to new information. We're starting with a premise that maybe we don't know everything, that it's possible we've misunderstood or made mistakes. Teachable people know how to ask for help, and they are marked with humility. Without teachability, there will be no growth, and without humility, there will be no victory.

Humility is the secret sauce for healthy relationships–whether we're talking about family, romance, work environments or social groups, humility helps every time. We talk about communication, trust, and honesty in relationships, but humility needs to also be at the top of that list. The world sees humility as weakness, but the Lord sees humility as wisdom.

When it comes to rejection, humility and teachability are especially useful. In order to renew our minds, we have to be willing to let go of the patterns of thought that have not been serving us well. We have to admit that what we have been doing isn't working, and commit to learning something new. We have to stop blaming our pain on other people and be willing to take responsibility for the things that we can do to change it.

One of the keys to gaining victory over rejection is to accept the premise that you have a narrative in your head that isn't always true. Rejection and the fear of rejection will always have a narrative for you that is negative. There will be a constant stream of thoughts in your mind offering explanations for what is happening around you–filling in blanks and jumping to conclusions.

We need to be less suspicious of other peoples agendas, and more suspicious of our own. The truth is, most people are doing their best and dealing with a lot. Most of the actions we take have more to do with us than anyone else–we're a pretty self-centred bunch. If you are entertaining a narrative that you are being rejected by everyone you see, you have a worldview that puts you at the centre. You're assuming everything is about you, and that's pride.

When you cultivate humility, it's easy to see that most things aren't about you at all and to start to give people the benefit of the doubt. Rejection and fear have no grace for the people around you, they are quick to judge and quicker to condemn. Humility has abundant grace for the people around you, and it even assumes the best. You can go from assuming the worst, to not just being neutral, but actually assuming the best about others. You won't always be right, but I can testify that assuming the best about others is a lot more freeing.

Curiosity

Curiosity is your best friend when you want to grow. It's such a powerful tool because it has no fear in it. Fear has a great imagination; it's always coming up with reasons to explain the world around you. Fear loves to fill in the blanks, to give a concrete connection between what you know and what you don't. For example, if someone you love is late arriving home, what is your first thought? Do you imagine they may have been in a terrible car accident and are lying unconscious in a hospital? This is a really common reaction.

One of the keys to gaining victory over rejection is to accept the premise that you have a narrative in your head that isn't always true.

The temptation is to take the first, easiest explanation but it is not the voice of God. When you encounter a mystery, resist the urge to explain it. Mystery makes us uncomfortable and God would rather have us uncomfortable in mystery than comfortable in fear. You don't need to have an answer for everything. You know the One who does, and that's enough.

Children are great at staying curious, their innocence and sense of wonder is inspiring to be around. They have a bent towards optimism, unless they have faced trauma already in their lives. I believe we are all born as optimists, and pessimism is the fruit of a broken world. If you have ever described yourself as a pessimist, or even a realist, it's time to let go of that identity and reengage with wonder and curiosity. Be okay with unanswered questions. When we really break it down, curiosity is possible when we trust someone bigger than us.

For a while I had a daycare in my home—while I was working in ministry, I set up this daycare as a bit of a side hustle to help pay the bills. Kind of like Paul and his tent making business, those of us in ministry have long been familiar with the concept of working one job to pay for the ability to work for the Kingdom. At times I would feel frustrated that I was "stuck" in the house with kids all day instead of doing the ministry that I felt called to, but there were so many treasures for me in that place of being stuck.

We're so quick to rush through seasons when God is asking us to slow down. Spending my days with 7 kids aged four and under gave me plenty of opportunities to observe the gift of wonder. I remember one particularly energetic 2-year-old, who had a great bond with me. He loved jumping off of whatever he could find, that was his favourite activity, next to dumping things out of bins of course.

What was interesting though was that this little guy had a complete lack of fear. At that age, he had not yet experienced anything but safe landings. If he jumped off something a bit too high, someone always caught him. He didn't care who, he didn't care how, he wasn't aware of what a person had to drop to catch him, he just knew that he always had a soft landing. It became a challenge for me, because he didn't wait to make sure I was watching when he jumped. He just jumped. That is the kind of childlike faith I want to grab hold of. I want to trust that God is going to give me a safe landing no matter how rough things look. Letting go of the fear attached to experiences that have hurt in the past, I want to embrace curiosity and wonder as I live in victory over rejection.

Hope

Hope is necessary for change. Without it, there's no motivation. Even a small amount of hope is enough to sustain you, as it's not so much about quantity as it is about quality. "Hope deferred makes the heart sick;" this is a Scripture that so quickly comes to mind when we are in pain. Yes, your soul says, that's me! My hope is deferred, I am heart sick. And it's true, but it's not the whole truth.

"Hope deferred makes the heart sick, but a desire fulfilled is a tree of life."

Proverbs 13:12

What this verse is saying is that what makes you ill is having your hope stolen. Not the thing you hope for, but the actual hope itself. Solomon was demonstrating that we can actually hope for a long time, but if our hope is gone, that's when we are losing the battle. If you've been rejected a lot in life, you know that hope is fleeting. You know how tough it is to believe that things can be different, to trust new people or to imagine a life where you don't live under the weight of rejection. You've tried everything you know to do, but you find yourself in the same place again.

Hope is not really useful unless it is enduring hope. If your hope dissipates at the first sign of challenge, it's not the high-quality kind of hope that is provided by the Lord. Study Scriptures about hope, ask the Holy Spirit to teach you about it, and talk to other people you know who have it. You can pray for God to just dunk you in it, but in my experience, it requires my own participation as well. I had to give up my right to be hopeless, be humble enough to admit I might be wrong, and curious enough to partner with the Holy Spirit and learn about hope from Him. You can see how all four of these tools work in unison and are powered by the Holy Spirit.

I'm asking you to stir up some hope once more, even if it's just a sliver. In order to renew your mind, you have to believe that your mind can be renewed. It's time to believe. Believe that it's not too late; believe that there is a version of your life where you have victory over rejection and fear and get to build healthy relationships. If you don't have any hope, I'd refer you back to humility. Is it possible that you're wrong?

Holy Spirit

Alright so you've got humility, you've got hope, you're engaging curiosity, and the last thing you need to renew your mind is the Holy Spirit. If you are a born again believer, you have Him living inside of you! That's the good news. Scripture talks about the renewing work of the Holy Spirit, and as believers we have the privilege of intimate relationship with Him. We can hear His voice, we can learn His nature, and we can feel His power and love.

One of His primary functions in a believer is to bring sanctification—to help us grow and mature and become more like Him. With the Holy Spirit inside of you, you can surrender every desire, thought and dream, allowing Him to guide you.

That kind of surrender means that in giving up our right to be right, we get His thoughts in exchange for ours. We get more of Him—more wisdom and revelation and love. Renewing your mind is not even possible without the Holy Spirit, because what would you be renewing your mind to?

> *"Do not be conformed to this world, but be transformed by the renewal of your mind, that by testing you may discern what is the will of God, what is good and acceptable and perfect."*
>
> *Romans 12:2*

This is our goal: to have our minds aligned with the will of God. After years of rejection wounds, our minds become conformed to the world, twisted into a worldview that has no element of the perfect will of God. We need help, and the Holy Spirit is well equipped. The goal we are aiming for is not that we will never be rejected again, but that we're secure even if we are rejected.

What other people choose to do is out of our control, and we are only responsible for our own actions. And the Holy Spirit is not under our control either, but what we do control is how much we surrender to Him. Will you give Him access to your habits, your thoughts, and your feelings? Will you trust Him with your pain, your questions, and your doubts? We get to decide how much ground we give the Lord in our own hearts and spirits.

Renewing Your Mind

Now that we have the four tools needed to renew our minds, let's take a look at what actually needs to happen. There has been invaluable information released over the last decade or so about how our brains like to build pathways over time, and that it is possible to change our thought patterns but it takes concentrated effort. I am no expert, I'm more like one of the mice in the experiment that can tell you what it's like. I would recommend reading Dr. Caroline Leaf's books if you want to dive further into the technical aspects of changing your thinking —she has done great work researching and educating people on *neuroplasticity*—the ability of our brain to change over time.

Automatic thinking is a phrase that simply describes our default way of thinking. The first step in making a change is recognizing where you are. The next time you start to feel discouraged, rejected, or fearful, take a step back and just notice what thoughts you're having. This can sometimes be the hardest step because we usually let our thoughts run and are unaware of where they're going.

If you can, slow down and take notice of what thoughts you are having—without judgement or trying to fix it right away. Write them down. After doing this a few times, when you have some of that data gathered and a better understanding of what thoughts lead up to the painful experiences and feelings of rejection, make some time to process together with the Holy Spirit.

While this is a very basic exercise, it's nonetheless one that I have found to be helpful quite often. Take a sheet of paper and make a line down the middle. On the left, write "Enemy's voice" and on the right, "God's voice". Start to make a list of all the thoughts you have when you feel rejected that are hurtful. It doesn't matter if they feel true. Spill them all out onto that paper.

Now pray and ask God to show you what He has to say. For each line that you've written in the first column, let Him respond in the second. When we've given so much space to the enemy in our thoughts, we need to be really intentional about also giving space to the Lord. If you're out of practice with hearing God, this might take some time, but it's worth it. Let Him speak. Honour

His words by writing them down and saying yes to them.

After you have your full sheet, I want you to do something that may sound a bit controversial. Look at those thoughts in the left column, and follow them out to the extreme. Look at where those thoughts are leading you to. What is the end game? Remember your enemy wants nothing more than to steal, kill and destroy.

The problem is that when we start to partner with these thoughts, they sound helpful. It feels like self-protection, like wisdom even. It sounds like logic. It is a slow downhill slope, and we can't always see where we're headed. But when you really get a good look at where these thoughts are leading you, you have to face just how ugly it is. These thoughts are not your friends; they are not helping you, and in fact they don't even originate in you. They are breadcrumbs from an enemy marching you to a death camp.

Repeat after me: *I cannot afford to think this way. I cannot afford to think this way.*

The cost of these thoughts is too high—it will cost you everything. It will not just stay at this level of pain that you can manage, it will spiral into something all-consuming. For me, this was a key phrase that stopped me from following that breadcrumb trail. I wrote it down; I even made it the lock screen on my phone for awhile. I shared it with a friend and asked her to remind me of it when I was struggling.

I encourage you to find your own key phrase if this one doesn't feel like a good fit for you. I am such a logical thinker…I would get stuck in my old thought patterns because they weren't actually lies. They were all true; they were things that had happened to me so it didn't seem like it was the enemy's voice at all. But when I followed them through to the extreme and saw the direction that they were taking me, I knew that I had to stop partnering with them. "I cannot afford to think this way," was a game-changer for me.

I also had the blessing of a counsellor who helped me to really see what the roots of my rejection lies were. We were able to unpack my childhood wounds and see the core beliefs that I adopted as a young girl around rejection. I chose to let go of those beliefs and to accept what God said about me instead. Just like in medicine, we need to treat the root cause and not the symptoms. The enemy loves distractions and wants you to focus on stopping other people from rejecting you. That's a symptom. The root cause is what you believe about yourself.

I looked for key Scriptures that I could also hold onto when things felt shaky and kept a list of those in my phone. I had another note on my phone, and still look at it from time to time. It has 5 key lies and truths that I was able to articulate around rejection. 5 things that felt true based on my experience, and the 5 responses of God to those things. I made a choice to believe His words even when they didn't feel true, and in time my emotions caught up to my thoughts.

I would pull those notes up in situations where I started to feel anxious and out of control. In group settings or work environments where I felt rejection was triggered, I pulled that note up and read the truths over and over. Even though they didn't exactly apply in that situation, I began to recognize the emotion I was feeling and applied the truth to it.

There are so many little excuses our brains will use to hang on to the old thought patterns; we need to have a plan of action when we want to make a change. I would also recommend having one or two trusted friends that you share these truths with. When we are struggling emotionally, most people mean well but say things that are really unhelpful. If you have a close friend, share with them what you're walking through, and let them know what truths you are focusing on in those moments you feel triggered.

I also think it's really important to practice saying these truths out loud. Our voices are powerful, and when this battle lives only in our heads it can feel somewhat secret. When we declare things out loud, there is an ownership and authority that helps cement our thinking. In "Christian-ese" we call these declarations.

Whether you're alone, or with a friend who understands, it's good to declare out loud the truths you've processed to incorporate them into your daily life. Stand in front of a mirror and practice your declarations. I made this a practice regularly, and I forced myself to do it even when my feelings didn't agree with the declaration. Even if I felt silly, or uncomfortable, or foolish. I pressed in because I wanted to see if words had more authority than feelings do.

On the other hand, it can also be really helpful to speak out loud the more negative thoughts that are in your head. We often entertain thoughts that we would never say out loud to ourselves, or anyone else. Allowing them to run through your head gives them a kind of secrecy, a way to hide and go unchecked. When you voice those thoughts out loud, you might be shocked at how negative and destructive they actually are. When you speak them out, you get to feel immediately when you do not actually agree with them. Sometimes that shock is what we need to stop entertaining the thoughts in our heads. If you would not want anyone else to hear you say it, is it really something you want to be thinking?

The worst thing that you can do when you're feeling rejected is isolate yourself. Loneliness is the enemy's sweet spot. He thrives there. Solitary confinement is the highest form of punishment we have in our society, other than the death penalty. When prisoners who have already been stripped of every freedom need to be punished further, they are thrown into solitary confinement. It was the same for ancient Israel - under the Mosaic covenant there were no jails or prisons. The most extreme punishment was to be cut off from your people—the offender would be forced to live outside the camp on their own. No help, no resources, no community. And this is what we impose on ourselves when we feel rejected!

The worst thing that you can do when you're feeling rejected is isolate yourself.

Again, the principle for victory is pretty obvious—do the opposite. If your default is to isolate when you're hurting, reach out to someone instead. Choose to be vulnerable rather than always showing a brave face. Start small, find one friend who loves you and text or call them the next time you feel triggered. The goal is not to ask them to fix you, the goal is to not be alone.

No one else is responsible for making you better, and no one else is able to. It is your work to do, but it is best done in community. This might take some trial and error—you might find that some people are really unhelpful to be around when you're feeling triggered by rejection. And that's okay, just keep trying. Look for people who are non-judgemental and have good boundaries. Look for people who know how to hear God and have demonstrated that they care about you.

Practicing these tools with the help of the Holy Spirit will renew your mind. He will also show you other things, ways to overcome old habits that are specific to you. With humility, curiosity, and hope, you will find freedom. God promises us to bring healing to every area of our lives when we surrender to Him. Listen to this Scripture where Paul is encouraging and teaching the Ephesians how to walk in love and see real change in their lives.

"Therefore do not become partners with them; for at one time you were darkness, but now you are light in the Lord. Walk as children of light (for the fruit of light is found in all that is good and right and true), and try to discern what is pleasing to the Lord. Take no part in the unfruitful works of darkness, but instead expose them. For it is shameful even to speak of the things that they do in secret. But when anything is exposed by the light, it becomes visible, for anything that becomes visible is light. Therefore it says, Awake, O sleeper, and arise from the dead, and Christ will shine on you."

Ephesians 5:7-12

The fear of rejection is faith in the wrong kingdom, and faith always grows fruit. Renewing your mind will not only stop the harvest of bad fruit in your life, but it will bring an abundance of good fruit, fruit that nourishes you and allows you to have healthy, thriving relationships. You also get to put a stop to generational cycles of rejection and fear in your lineage. When you cut down this giant in your own life, you're taking away its authority to gain ground in the lives of your children. And that, Beloved, is a gift of great value.

8

Identity

The thoughts we think about who we are and who God is form many of our behaviours and habits. It affects every area of our lives, and it's hard to measure the impact of who we think we are. When rejection is part of our history, our identity can be formed and shaped by those temporary circumstances rather than our eternal identity.

Since I have been writing this book, I discovered a situation that was a trigger for me from rejection I experienced years ago. It was a repeating scenario, something that happened every year in a friendship that means a lot to me. This year when the reminder came up again, I realized I still had some pain around it. I set aside some time and took my Bible and journal to a quiet space. I did all the things I'm suggesting to you in this book—I engaged humility, curiosity, hope and the Holy Spirit.

This can look a bunch of different ways, but for journalling I like to of course pray first and connect with God. I read my Bible and spend a bit of time in worship, and invite the Holy Spirit to speak to me. The Bible tells us that the way we enter His courts is with praise. Yes, we have the Holy Spirit inside of us and can hear Him anytime. But I find that intentional connection and becoming aware of His Presence is always helpful when I want to hear His voice clearly.

After I have that connection opened up, I start journalling and ask some questions in each of those three areas. For humility, this usually sounds like, "Is there any way I've been wrong in my thinking about this rejection experience?" And then I listen and write out what the Holy Spirit shows me. Then I move to curiosity, which can sound like, "I wonder if there's a different way to look at this," and write that down. Give some space for the Holy Spirit to speak to each question, and don't be surprised if He brings other questions to mind.

This curiosity naturally leads me to hope. Hope sounds like: "What would it look like to be in this situation and not feel rejected?" Really start to imagine what that would be like. What needs to change for you to get from here to there? Are there mindsets you need to let go of? Is there something you need to communicate with those people? Write it down.

After I've gone through each of these things, I give some space to examine my own heart and work through repentance and forgiveness. I ask the Holy Spirit to show me if there's anything I need to repent for. In this scenario, for me it's something I've been aware of and worked through before. But when I asked the Holy Spirit to search my heart again, I saw that I had really valued this person's opinion of me more than I valued God's opinion of me, and I needed to repent for that.

I also looked at forgiveness, and saw that I have forgiven this person and affirmed my decision to release them from any debt or punishment and release them in Jesus' name. That is the kind of mental and spiritual "work" it takes to achieve victory over rejection. For some of our experiences, after completing these steps, we see that it was not rejection at all, and the pain from that wound is healed. Sometimes the Holy Spirit releases incredible revelation and your feelings immediately line up with Heaven, and when you think about that experience, you no longer feel pain.

Sometimes there is still residual pain from rejection, and you recognize circumstances that trigger that pain. This can happen even when you've been doing the work and are open to change. It's in this sweet spot that we get to explore our understanding of our identity. Identity is something that we are continually learning about. I've been around a lot of mature leaders during my time in ministry, and I still don't know anyone who doesn't need to continuously grow in their understanding of identity. I'm not saying that this is where you start to work on it, I'm sure you've heard teaching on it and have given thought to it before. What I'm saying is that if you're feeling stuck when it comes to rejection, if you've tried everything and still get triggered, then you need to invest some more time and energy into exploring your identity in Christ.

We are all familiar with feelings of insecurity. At different times in life, we feel insecure about our bodies, our skills, or our popularity. It might bubble up more often around specific people or in specific places. Insecurity feels like anxiety, fear, and nerves. It makes us do things we don't want to do—lying, running away, or making fun of other people.

When we pay attention to our insecurities, we can narrow down the areas where we need correction. Your insecurities are the areas where you have embraced a false identity. If you are insecure about your looks or your body, it's because you have been looking to find your identity and your value in your looks and your body. If you are insecure about your job, how much money you make, or a promotion, it's because that's where you have been finding identity. Maybe you worry about being accepted by certain people or groups - whatever triggers insecurity in you is the area you have been looking to for safety.

Your insecurities are the areas where you have embraced a false identity.

Pay attention to your insecurities and repent for them. The only place we rightly find security is in Jesus. Everything else is an idol. When we talk about identity in the church today, we also need to give some direction for how to apply it. Beloved, this is the application of our identity in Christ. We pinpoint our insecurities and determine our trigger points, and then we repent for idolizing people or worldly values. Allowing the Holy Spirit this access to your heart is so important for maturity. This is what it means to love the discipline of the Lord! Psalm 51 is my heart's cry, in the old Keith Green version.

> *"Create in me a clean heart, O God;*
> *And renew a right spirit within me.*
> *Cast me not away from thy presence, O Lord*
> *And take not thy Holy Spirit from me.*
> *Restore unto me the joy of thy salvation;*
> *And renew a right spirit within me."*

If our identity is not in any of these things—what we do, how we look, what we have or who we're with—what is our identity? The world today says that our identity is whatever we choose. You can be male or female, straight or gay—you can identify as whatever you want and other people will accept it. The world defines identity with feelings. If you have male parts but feel like a female, your identity is female. If you have female parts but feel attracted to other females, your identity is lesbian. The world has made an idol out of feelings. Feelings above truth is the cry of this generation, and it is grieving the heart of God.

There are literally hundreds of verses about your identity in the Bible. He must've known that we would need a few reminders! When we think about identity, there are three areas we should consider to help us frame what it is: our created design, our redeemed humanity, and our identity in Christ. Who am I? This is a basic question that we all must answer, and as Christians it should look different than the world around us. You are not your feelings. You are not your temptations. And you are not your failures or successes. You are who God says you are.

Created Design

Your created design is that you were made in the image of God. We go way back to the Garden of Eden and see that man (and woman) were created to display the image of God, and He called us good. You look at the Psalms and see how there was intelligent design in our creation; that there was intention and love and care in how we were formed in our mother's wombs. You were not a random accident, you were not the result of cells multiplying and evolving on their own, and you were not created and then abandoned to a broken world full of sin and sickness. You were created in God's image to reflect His glory.

This is your original design, as well as the design of every human being that ever has or ever will live. This part of your identity is not conditional to ethnicity, gender, or any other distinction. It does not change with your beliefs—whether you are Christian or follow any other religion. Each one of us was created in love, by love, and for love. We were created in God's image, to reflect His glory. This is who you are.

Redeemed Humanity

As a Christian, you are also more than your original design; you have been redeemed by the sacrifice of Christ on the cross. This means that every mistake, every sin and every part of you that you don't like has been redeemed. You have been fully restored to relationship with God and have been adopted as His child. You are a rightful heir to every inheritance through Christ. You are loved by Him, valued by Him, cared for by Him, protected by Him, and provided for by Him. This is your current reality, and there is no danger of losing it in any way.

You came from Him and are going back to Him—you will be in Heaven for eternity. You have access to God's Presence here and now and have the Holy Spirit living inside of you. This is who you are.

Identity in Christ

This is the part most talked about in the church today, and as a logic focused person I have found it hard to theologically grasp the meaning of that phrase. Does it mean that I am non-existent, that accepting Jesus as my Saviour completely replaces me? Does it mean that I have no distinct personality or characteristics, that I am dead and He now lives through me? I don't think that's exactly right. We still are created individual human beings, and each of us reflect His glory in a unique way. Our gifts, personality, quirks, passions and strengths are all a unique expression and don't need to be hidden or killed.

What it means to have our identity in Christ is that we accept Him as our Lord and Saviour. It means that God sees us the same way He sees Jesus, that we are known as He is, and that we are loved as He is. Jesus is the Son of God, righteous and holy, He is blameless and pure, He is glorified and sitting at the right hand of God. Jesus is perfectly loved, accepted, and chosen. He has no faults or sin in Him, and He has authority over every enemy in the spiritual realm. Jesus is victorious over sin, sickness and death. He has direct access to God and is one with the Holy Spirit.

To accept that our identity is in Christ is to accept that our sinful nature is dead. We are hidden in Him, meaning that we are united with Him and cannot be separated. In the book of Ephesians alone, the phrase "in Christ" is used 36 times! It is a growing awareness of our union with Christ that helps us to grasp our identity. This is who you are. Here is a poetic piece of writing soaked in theology about our identity:

"Blessed be the God and Father of our Lord Jesus Christ, who has blessed us in Christ with every spiritual blessing in the heavenly places, even as he chose us in him before the foundation of the world, that we should be holy and blameless before him. In love he predestined us for adoption to himself as sons through Jesus Christ, according to the purpose of his will, to the praise of his glorious grace, with which he has blessed us in the Beloved. In him we have redemption through his blood, the forgiveness of our trespasses, according to the riches of his grace, which he lavished upon us, in all wisdom and insight making known to us the mystery of his will, according to his purpose, which he set forth in Christ as a plan for the fullness of time, to unite all things in him, things in heaven and things on earth.

In him we have obtained an inheritance, having been predestined according to the purpose of him who works all things according to the counsel of his will, so that we who were the first to hope in Christ might be to the praise of his glory. In him you also, when you heard the word of truth, the gospel of your salvation, and believed in him, were sealed with the promised Holy Spirit, who is the guarantee of our inheritance until we acquire possession of it, to the praise of his glory."

Ephesians 1:3-14

Isn't that beautiful? This is who you are, and this is a great antidote against rejection and the fear of rejection. When you are convinced of your true identity, there are so many benefits. The fruit of the Spirit - love, joy, peace, patience, kindness, goodness, faithfulness, gentleness and self-control—are multiplied. This fruit allows you to grow in every circumstance.

Knowing your identity helps you to build healthy relationships with others, because you will have healthy boundaries and be able to communicate well. It creates opportunities for you to encourage others and share the truth of the gospel with others. When you're sure of your identity you are able to avoid the traps that the enemy sets for you and destroy his plans for your life.

Triumphal Procession

The truth is, the enemy knows your identity better than you do. He doesn't need convincing, feelings, or evidence; he already knows what God says is true—he just doesn't like it. Much like a spider, he's more scared of you than you are of him, and he plays on our fear that we are vulnerable to him.

"But thanks be to God, who in Christ always leads us in triumphal procession, and through us spreads the fragrance of the knowledge of him everywhere. For we are the aroma of Christ to God among those who

are being saved and among those who are perishing."

2 Corinthians 2:14-15

I've always loved the language of Paul's writing. He's poetic, dramatic, and passionate. But some of his original intention can be lost or misinterpreted, unless we look at what it meant to the people who first read his letters. The passage above contains beautiful poetic language that was written to the church in Corinth, but what does it mean?

When you're sure of your identity you are able to avoid the traps that the enemy sets for you and destroy his plans for your life.

The triumphal procession he's talking about was a common practice in Rome. When the Roman army conquered new territory, they would return with a victory parade in Rome to celebrate. First in the parade would be the captives—the enemy captured and in chains, marched through the streets for all to see that they have been incapacitated and would soon be killed. The enemy may be able to make noise and mock the people, but they were clearly conquered. Next in line would be the priests, carrying censers filled with sweet incense. The aroma from the incense would waft through the city, a signal to the people that victory was won, and the emperor was present.

Next in line was the emperor, sitting on a tall chariot, proud and victorious. There would be a slave beside him, holding a gold crown above his head and continuously whispering in his ear "respice". The Latin word respice means "look behind," and would remind the victor that he was mortal, that even in this victory he should remain humble. Just behind the emperor, grateful citizens from the city would join in the procession, singing of the victory. They had smelled the aroma and had followed it out onto the streets where they witnessed the captive enemy, and sang praises as they followed the victorious emperor.

That really changes this passage, doesn't it? Or at least sheds light on Paul's encouragement here. We are this aroma to the world—a signal that the Victor, Christ, is present! Our actions and words cause people to join the procession of God, to praise Him and celebrate His presence. And this picture of the enemy—captured, chained up, but still making noise is so true of our current reality - Christ has conquered our enemy and he will soon be completely defeated. We need to remember that he may be making noise, but we don't need to fear him because Christ has the victory!

So let's be the aroma of Christ! Let's behave in such a way that we are drawing people to Christ by speaking love and hope. Let our lives be a signal to the world that the enemy is conquered, and Christ is present with us. This begins with confidence in our identity—we are not captured, walking in chains and unable to find freedom. We are the free ones, the wild ones dancing behind the King and reflecting His glory.

Spiritual Warfare

When you are facing lies from the enemy about your identity and temptations to find security in other places it can be an intense spiritual battle. One of the great strategies we have from the Lord when we're in spiritual warfare is to engage the armour of God. This is found in Ephesians 6, but in our day and age, it takes a bit more exploring to really see the picture of what the author was trying to communicate.

Most of us have never seen battle armour up close. We're familiar with images of muscly guys in camouflage holding large guns, but soldiers during the time of the New Testament looked much different. Paul was in prison in Rome when he wrote Ephesians, so he was likely staring at a Roman soldier when he wrote these words.

"Finally, be strong in the Lord and in the strength of his might. Put on the whole armour of God, that you may be able to stand against the schemes of the devil. For we do not wrestle against flesh and blood, but against the rulers, against the authorities, against the cosmic powers over this present darkness, against the spiritual forces of evil in the heavenly places. Therefore take up the whole armour of God, that you may be able to withstand in the evil day, and having done all, to stand firm. Stand therefore, having fastened on the belt of truth, and having put on the breastplate of righteousness, and, as shoes for your feet, having put on the readiness given by the gospel of peace. In all circumstances take up the shield of faith, with which you can extinguish all the flaming darts of the evil one; and take the helmet of salvation, and the sword of the Spirit, which is the word of God, praying at all times in the Spirit, with all prayer and supplication. To that end, keep alert with all perseverance, making supplication for all the saints, and also for me, that words may be given to me in opening my mouth boldly to proclaim the mystery of the gospel, for which I am an ambassador in chains, that I may declare it boldly, as I ought to speak."

Ephesians 6:10-20

The apostle wrote this beautiful letter detailing the

inheritance that is available to us in Christ and then encouraged the Ephesians to move from darkness to light. He was showing them how to let go of their past and partner with the God who makes all things new. And then before signing off, he looked at the soldier holding him captive, the one who came to steal his freedom, and saw a practical example of what the Church needed. This is what we need. This is what is available to us, what God has provided that stops the enemy from stealing, killing and destroying.

The first thing he mentions is the belt of truth. Belts were not common at this time, not part of everyday wear. They were action items. A belt was preparation for combat. Fastening a belt meant that you were aware of the action you were walking into. I love that it's the first item on the list too—everything else falls apart if we're not secure in truth. It doesn't matter if you have a big sword…if your underwear falls down in the middle of battle, you're vulnerable! Truth is vital, and should be our priority.

Next is the breastplate of righteousness. It's a bit of a misnomer, because the breastplates the soldiers wore actually covered them front and back. Righteousness is about holy living, about staying away from the things that lead us out of God's presence, and we're encouraged to keep our lives pure, both in the past and the future. Jesus covers all our past mistakes, all of our sin, hallelujah! And He enables us to make better choices in our future.

What's additionally interesting about this piece of armour is that it goes from the neck down to the thighs. Our neck is symbolic of decision making, our freedom to choose. Our thighs are symbolic of flesh—passion and strength. God has freely provided this protection - for our past and our future, for every decision we make and temptation we have, He not only calls us to righteousness but He makes a way.

History tells us that these Roman soldiers had their battle

shoes fitted with strong, sharp nails in the bottom to give them traction. What I think the Lord is saying here is that it is His peace is a foundation that allows us to stand when things get slippery. When we cultivate a habit of peace in our lives, we are ready at any moment to hold our ground. It doesn't matter if the enemy is slimy, if the ground is not steady, or if other people have made a mess in your path. Peace enables us to stand firm.

Next up is the shield of faith. I used to picture more of a cartoonish little shield that you could whip around and block an attack with. Nope. These Roman shields were 2.5 x 4 ft, and they were significant and stable. They covered your whole body, and they were sturdy wood, wrapped in leather. What the soldiers would do is they would wet the shields down as they went into battle. Because they knew their enemy, they knew the tactics that would be used against them, and one of them was flaming darts. Their preparation made them flameproof. They might still feel the impact of an arrow hitting their shields, but it wouldn't do any permanent damage.

And here's the things about shields—they're most powerful when they're used in community. Soldiers would line up, placing their shields edge-to-edge so that there was no opening, no entrance for the enemy's fiery darts, and inch their way forward to take new ground. If they worked together in this way, they were unstoppable!

Moving forward, taking new territory, steadily and in unison they would gain victory after victory. This, my beloved, is a picture of the church as we're meant to be. We are meant to stand next to each other, soaking our faith in the water of the Holy Spirit that makes us completely impervious to the enemy's attacks. We may feel the impact as we come against opposition, but we won't get permanently wounded when we keep our faith up.

One key thing about the shield was that soldiers would mark

their name and unit on the back where they could see it. It was their version of "dog tags" as we know them today. They inscribed into their shield of faith their identity, and had it up in front of them where they could see it in the middle of the battle. Our identity is so often the first and greatest attack we face, so let's be confident before we enter combat of who we are and Who we belong to. No matter what circumstances and challenges we are facing, our identity as His Beloved does not change.

Helmet of salvation—without it, you're dead. That's the whole point of a helmet, right? To protect your most vulnerable part, your head and your face. The implication here is that if we don't know that we're saved, we're very easily taken out. If you are unsure that Christ died to save you, if you doubt that He really loves you, if you're wavering on whether or not you belong to Him, it's really easy for the enemy to sneak in and do some damage to your spirit and your life. I haven't ever doubted my salvation (thankfully), but I have doubted God's love for me. Anytime I make my circumstances bigger than God, I start to doubt His love. Any time you are doubting God's love for you, you are taking off that helmet and making yourself vulnerable.

The last thing we need is the sword of the Spirit, the Word of God. Roman soldiers actually carried two offensive weapons. In addition to their long spear, they also had a short combat sword, which is the one that Paul focuses on in this passage. This was a double-edged dagger, meant for stabbing in close contact. When all their defences were exhausted, and the short burst of hand-to-hand combat came upon them, they would pull out this sharp sword and use it to kill the enemy—fast and strong.

The word used in Scripture here for "word" of God is rhema. You may be familiar with the two Greek words logos and rhema that we translate to "word" of God. Logos refers to the written word, and rhema to the spoken word. Rhema is about the Holy

Spirit speaking to us, and in this case, we're called to use the things that the Holy Spirit has spoken, to take out our enemy. When the rhema word of God is spoken, our enemy cannot stand. When we declare His truth, when we prophesy things on earth as they are in heaven, we disable the enemy.

Beloved, this armour of God is no joke! There is so much here that speaks to the lovingkindness of a God who never meant for us to walk into battle empty-handed. The good news of the gospel of Christ is that He has provided all of this, it is all free for us to take. This armour is who He is for us—it's not something we fight for, or perform our way into—this is provided by Jesus. He is our salvation, our peace, our faith, our identity, our righteousness, and He is truth itself. We only have to be aware of what we carry in order to participate in the rich inheritance we have as children of God. May every one of us go forward, prepared to take new ground and live in victory!

9

Preventing Rejection

The goal of gaining victory over rejection is not to stop it from happening, but to know that you will be okay if and when it does happen again. We want to fully heal our wounds from the past, renew our minds and make any changes that we need to in order to truly be walking in victory. This is a mindset shift that is necessary for moving on, otherwise you will be moving towards the wrong goal.

Once you've worked through repentance, forgiveness, and started the work of renewing your mind, you'll want to put strategies in place for how you're going to handle events in the future that feel like rejection. If you fail to plan, you plan to fail. Knowing what your triggers are and what tools you have is a great place to start.

When we talk about preventing rejection, what we are really aiming for is preventing rejection from stealing from our future. Putting the work in now means that when a crisis hits you are already prepared. It's kind of like purchasing insurance—there is a cost to it now, but you have peace of mind knowing that if something bad happens, you have a plan for how to deal with it.

The work that you are doing now to pursue health and wholeness will pay off. Taking the time to let God heal your wounds, to forgive others and renew your mind means that you can have peace when you need to practice those things in the future. Anytime we align ourselves with the mind of Christ and allow ourselves to be molded and shaped, changed and transformed, our Father in Heaven is incredibly proud. We have a great cloud of witnesses cheering us on!

One of the most beloved characters in the Bible has to be David. Shepherd boy and charismatic king, David wrote close to half of the Psalms that we still read today. One of the reasons he is so admired by people from across generations is his authenticity. David expressed a wide range of emotions in the psalms that he wrote and clearly shared those feelings with the Lord. We don't like his story because it was perfect; we like his story because he was honest. If we never see a model of how to make mistakes and recover, we won't have any resiliency. David is a great example of a man with a great calling who loved the Lord and made some really grievous mistakes. We can learn from him about how to cultivate enduring faith that doesn't fold at the first sign of resistance.

When I read stories in the Bible, I'm always curious about the thought lives of the characters. What was going through Peter's brain when he saw Jesus feed the 5,000? What was Joseph thinking when his brothers sold him into slavery? What was David telling himself when he faced so many setbacks before becoming king? The thoughts we entertain are much more revealing than the actions we take. I always understand people much better when I ask a few questions about how they see things and why they make the choices they do.

When we talk about preventing rejection, what we are really aiming for is preventing rejection from stealing from our future.

David was the second king in the history of Israel as a nation. He reigned from 1010 - 970 BC. He was anointed at the age of 12, but he didn't take the throne until he was 30 years old. That's 18 years of waiting. A child could be conceived, birthed, and grown to adulthood in the time that David waited to step into the promise God gave him. I don't think that's an accident. I believe God values maturity and will prioritize our development over our desire for acceleration.

A lot of times we want to fast forward through the process because we don't have the faith that God's promises will be fulfilled. We want to speed up because we don't actually believe God will come through. If we did have the faith, we wouldn't feel the need to fast forward. If you find yourself praying for God to speed up the season you're in, try shifting your prayers to asking Him to help you learn everything you need to in your current season. Ask the Holy Spirit to show you how you can partner with what He's doing in your life. You might be surprised about how quickly things start to change.

If you've read the story of King David, mostly in 1 & 2 Samuel and 1 & 2 Chronicles, you'll know that David didn't wait idly for God to go to work for him. He partnered with the promise even when the people around him didn't approve, or more accurately, were actively trying to sabotage him. David had a great understanding of his identity, and was not taken out by the people or circumstances around him. He was shaken for sure, as we read in the Psalms, but not destroyed. Sometimes at the beginning of a psalm, you can read the context David gives for the circumstances he was in while he wrote that particular Psalm. When you match it up with the stories from Scripture, you get a good idea of what David was thinking at specific times in the story.

As a 12-year-old, he was plucked off of the field with the sheep and anointed to be king. I don't know many 12-year-olds that could handle that pressure, but David did. At 17, he stepped up and defeated Goliath, doing what no other man could do, but he still was not given the throne. At 27, he had led the army to victory after victory, but instead of being acknowledged for his victories, he was persecuted and attacked by the man who had his job. At 30, David finally takes the throne but it wasn't all smooth sailing from there. There was adultery, murder, parenting struggles, wins and losses. There was mourning and dancing. David was a king, but he was also a man and had to face the reality of sin, death, and sorrow that is part of this broken world.

In addition to his authenticity, one of David's great strengths was his desire for intimacy with the Lord. He valued the presence of God in his life so much that he prioritized it. A lot of times we talk about what we value, but our actions don't match it. We want to want a relationship with God, but we don't do anything that reflects it. We like the idea of spending time with God and know the benefit it has, but we allow other things to take priority.

We all do this, myself included! It's called being double-minded, when we have two conflicting desires or values and it requires sanctification with the help of the Holy Spirit to resolve that conflict within us. When we recognize that double-mindedness, it's good to invite the Holy Spirit to align our minds with His and to make choices that agree with our true desire. We often have to act on our thoughts before our feelings align with them.

One of the famous stories about David is his affair with Bathsheba. It's a tragic tale where we see our hero spiral out into a string of shameful sin. He takes another man's wife to bed, gets her pregnant, and then has her husband killed. Not his best moment. And it seems to come out of left field; David, the humble king who waited respectfully to take the throne from his predecessor, the one who slayed the giant and defended his country. Why did he suddenly slip into this negative spiral? We actually have a great but subtle clue from Scripture, one that we might be tempted to skip over. Let's take a look at the beginning of this part of his story.

> *"In the spring of the year, the time when kings go out to battle, David sent Joab, and his servants with him, and all Israel. And they ravaged the Ammonites and besieged Rabbah. But David remained at Jerusalem. It happened, late one afternoon, when David arose from his couch and was walking on the roof of the king's house, that he saw from the roof a woman bathing; and the woman was very beautiful."*

1 Samuel 11:1-2

This is the moment David sees Bathsheba and starts to lose control. We see that it is the time of year when kings go out to battle, and where is David? He's resting on his couch in the afternoon. I don't think this author is pointing out David's apparent laziness, I think he is highlighting an identity issue.

David has forgotten his true identity as the king of the nation, and has chosen to let someone else take over what is his authority and responsibility. He lost his focus and probably partnered with some kind of lie about who he was.

We often have to act on our thoughts before our feelings align with them.

The enemy doesn't want us to engage with these lies just to mess with our heads and emotions, he's actually trying to get us to change our behaviour. If David doesn't believe that he's the King of Israel, then he might not think that he's capable of winning, or worse, that it doesn't even matter if he's there or not. Maybe he thinks that there's someone else who can do it better or that he might mess it up. Whatever the lie was, it got him to stay home when he should have been at war. It opened the door to things that should never have been opened, and caused catastrophic consequences for him and everyone around him. David forgot who he was, and it led to death.

That's not the end of his story, though it did take some time to recover. It required another voice speaking in to his situation, someone he was accountable to that helped bring him out of the pit he had dug. His friend with a strong prophetic gift called him out. We all need a friend like Nathan! With a word from the Lord, Nathan reminded him of who he was.

> *"Nathan said to David, You are the man! Thus says the Lord, the God of Israel, I anointed you king over Israel, and I delivered you out of the hand of Saul. And I gave you your master's house and your master's wives into your arms and gave you the house of Israel and of Judah. And if this were too little, I would add to you as much more."*

1 Samuel 12:7-8

God intervenes and reminds David that He chose him to be king and had already provided wives for him. And He reminds David of who He is, that He's a God who will meet our needs and provide what we desire. He tears down the lies David had embraced and restores his identity. This is what God will do for us, if we're humble and teachable.

When we allow Him room to speak, He can correct every ounce of double-mindedness within us. Even after this monumental failure and his restoration, David still has ups and downs throughout the rest of his life. He makes some big mistakes in how he parents his kids, but he also sees a lot of victories.

What you'll see over and over again throughout the Psalms is David's desire for the Presence of God. His pull towards intimacy with the Lord is unmatched, and it's something I want to grow in. What I've found though is that this kind of intimacy cannot be accomplished as a task, it can only grow as we allow ourselves to be loved by Him. Prayer, worship, Bible reading—all of these are good and are ways that you can connect with God. But they are most fruitful when done out of love.

The greatest way to invest your time is by letting God love you, whether that is through spiritual disciplines or in a completely different way. The more you let Him love you, the more you will want to love Him. Time spent this way will never be wasted, it's always an investment, even if you don't feel an immediate benefit (though you usually do).

David cultivated this intimacy by letting the Lord love him and speak to his identity. He was accountable to people he could trust and was teachable. When he did make some pretty big mistakes, he didn't allow them to derail his entire future. David navigated ups and downs, circumstances both in and out of his control.

David was one of the few kings of Israel to leave a positive legacy and move the nation closer to the Lord, setting up his son well to take over the throne and build on the foundation he created. It seems that David was prepared for his life of ups and downs, that he had some kind of plan or strategy for how to navigate the different situations he would find himself in.

When I was coming out of a really difficult season, I decided I needed a plan as well. When you've been defeated by rejection so many times, it feels like you are getting continually knocked out of a boxing match. If you do what you've always done, you'll get what you always do. Our brains operate on auto pilot most of the time—we aren't actively choosing, rather just doing what we did before.

As I was doing the work of renewing my mind, I decided to make a plan of other things I could do that would be different responses to rejection or the fear of rejection. I decided to experiment for a month, even though it didn't totally make sense to me I was desperate to stop feeling like I was bruised and bloody from that boxing ring. I even decided to suspend logic, just for a month, and no longer accept any argument in my brain that didn't sound like love.

I had been so stuck in logic; it was as though I had built a house there and refused to budge. I was so focused on the fact that I had been rejected that I couldn't entertain any thoughts that were not in that same spirit. I literally could not comprehend thoughts that conflicted with rejection. But it was not serving me well It had sent me down a deep spiral of fear, depression, anxiety, and suicidal thoughts. So I made this temporary commitment: if and when I had those thoughts, I would stop and immediately say out loud, "I cannot afford to think this way."

It was a key phrase that felt safe to me, because I wasn't saying that I hadn't been rejected, and it didn't mean that I had to deny my experience or the ways I had been hurt. I was, however, finally acknowledging that dwelling on those thoughts would come at a huge cost—a cost I could no longer afford. I was, quite literally, close to death, and too much longer in that place would have cost me everything. I cannot afford to think this way was my mantra for a month. I had to make it the wallpaper on my phone lock screen, because it happened so often throughout each day and felt completely foreign that I needed a constant reminder.

Another thing you can do is set a reminder on your phone for intervals throughout the day, and put a key phrase in the text of the reminder. You'll get a notification that reminds you of what you're choosing to think. I also took some time when I was feeling pretty safe and connected to the Lord to come up with a list of things I could do differently. Again, my high value for logic and truth made it tricky to "just be positive" or "don't worry about it"—the kind of strategies we sometimes use in the church to encourage each other.

Those things work for some people, but I needed strategies that were also true for me in my circumstances, thoughts that didn't deny my experience but also held God's truth in the highest place. The great thing is, each of us are uniquely and wonderfully created by this same God, and He is a genius. He knows exactly which keys are needed to unlock the places we are stuck and get us to higher ground.

Draw close to Him, give Him room to speak, and ask Him to show you the keys that you need. Ask Him for Scriptures that will bring revelation. The Word of God is alive and active. One of my favourites at that time was Philippians—this verse comes right after a promise that the peace of God will rest on you.

"Finally, brothers and sisters, whatever is true,
whatever is noble, whatever is right, whatever is pure,

*whatever is lovely, whatever is admirable - if anything
is excellent or praiseworthy - think about such things."*

Philippians 4:8

I memorized this Scripture, I wrote it out, and I even created a pretty canvas and put it up above my fireplace. After I had a few of these things in place—key verses, key thoughts—I made a list of things I would do differently. Whenever I felt "triggered," I would take an action that was in the opposite spirit of what I was feeling. I mean, hello, uncomfortable. That month was the most uncomfortable and unsure I have ever been. Remember, change is always uncomfortable!

While much of my focus was centred on renewing my mind, I also started to choose different actions. I made a small list of things that I would do differently just for the sake of trying something different. My list included things like simply staying in a social situation. When you're used to hiding, simply not leaving the room is a drastic change! I decided I didn't have to feel good, I just had to choose a different action. Be uncomfortable, feel upset, cry, but don't leave the room.

I also chose two people who felt somewhat safe to share this with. I sent them the key phrases I had worked on, and I gave them permission to remind me of those if they saw me struggling. It can be really humbling to ask for help in this way, but accountability is a good thing! As long as you're not asking them to do the work for you, it's good to ask for help. No one should be working harder on these changes than you are.

Another thing I tried was to envision how safe I am in God's Presence. The thing about rejection is that it makes you feel extremely unsafe. You might feel vulnerable, open to deadly wounds, exposed, and ashamed. There are so many Scriptures about how safe God is. He's a tower to hide in; He's a rock to build on; He's a wing spread over you. The Psalms are full of this imagery, and I started to picture these things when I felt triggered by rejection or fear. I trained myself so that when I feel unsafe in a social situation I now naturally start to picture a large wing spread over me and tucking me in. There is no safer place to be than in God's Presence!

One of the hardest changes I made was to start assuming the best about other people. I had spent so long assuming the worst, predicting rejection around every corner, because at least half the time I was right. It may have been justified, but it came at such a high cost. When I decided to spend that month choosing different actions, I knew this would have to be a big one. And I'll be honest, it felt ridiculous. I went to the extreme. I decided that even if someone came up to me, said "I hate you," and punched me in the face, I would assume the best. I would choose a thought like, "I bet they mistook me for someone else." I would assume it wasn't about me at all. I practiced these extreme assumptions every day for a month.

This was a key to transformation for me. It's been a few years now, and I find it difficult to remember what it was really like when I used to assume the worst. I do remember being suspicious of everyone I interacted with. I could find a way for every word, text, or action to be interpreted as rejection. I assumed everything was about me and everyone thought I was the worst. It was exhausting. I remember feeling drained after every social gathering, and fearful and anxious of everything on the calendar.

There was nothing anyone could actually do or say to win my trust. When I started to assume the best, I really just felt silly. I felt like I would be taken advantage of and would be hurt again. It made no logical sense, but with a one-month time limit I decided the experiment was worth it.

The first few days of doing all these things was really difficult.

It did not feel good. It did not make anything better. Honestly, I was hoping I could make it through the 30 days and forever use that as evidence that my feelings were right and rejection would always be my identity. My feelings were not magically changing, and I did not see any great breakthrough. But sometimes the best breakthroughs happen slowly behind the scenes. I did not do it perfectly either. It was an imperfect process of falling into old patterns and then choosing to try again. God is so much more okay with a messy process than we are.

I would love to tell you that a month later I was cured. That I woke up on day 30 and it was suddenly easy. But that's not quite how it happened. What would be more accurate to say is that I was angry.

At the end of the month, I saw the truth of how much the enemy had been stealing from me through rejection and fear. I saw how so much of my life had been spent chained up by these emotions and thoughts, and that I had been duped by the lies. I was mad. And I was also mad that there wasn't a better solution! I wanted to be able to blame someone other than myself— perhaps the people who had rejected me, or God, for letting it happen. I wanted someone else to be responsible. But the truth is, after 30 days of making those changes, I saw just how much I was responsible for. I realized how much was actually in my control, and that there was no shortcut to victory.

It felt like it was taking so much energy and humility to make those changes every day in my thoughts and my actions, when I wanted someone else to just change my feelings. And I was scared that it would be a lifelong battle of living that way. It takes a lot of energy to change, but it takes a lot of energy to stay in an unhealthy state. They're both hard, and we get to choose which kind of hard we want to live with. I was not able to gloat and hold on to my justifications and logic. I could not go back to living in the constant pain. I could only go forward.

Preventing rejection had so much more to do with me than it did with defending against any kind of outside enemy. It did get easier over time, and these tools and thoughts have become as natural as the other ones used to be. I no longer live in fear or suspicion of every person and every social situation. I actually do naturally assume the best about other people.

I realized how much was actually in my control, and that there was no shortcut to victory.

I do sometimes still feel triggered and need to take a step back and consciously choose what is uncomfortable. But these tools have helped me transform into a different person. I really do think completely differently than I used to. And my feelings did catch up to the rest of me. The emotions followed, over time, and imperfectly. I think in the past if you had asked me what my biggest fear was, I would have told you it was being rejected or being alone. It was the worst thing I could imagine, and I would have done everything possible to prevent that pain.

Now, I can honestly say that that doesn't scare me. I have been rejected since then and probably will be again. It might hurt, but it won't destroy me. It won't actually change anything about my future, my identity, or my value. And now, I'm free to actually start loving the people in front of me.

10

Friends & Family

No matter how many broken relationships and stories of rejection you have in your past, there are also people who have stuck by you. They may not have done it perfectly, but they have tried to support you through all the challenges you've faced. There are people who love you and want you to succeed. Their faces are probably coming to mind right now, and you can likely recall some times when they have reached out and tried to help.

Maybe there have been some friends and family who were watching from a distance as you navigated the challenges and roadblocks that come along with rejection, fear, and social anxiety. It is really tough to face rejection. It is also really tough to support someone who is facing rejection. Its effects are far-reaching and ripple out to the people around us—but we can get so focused on our inner world that we fail to see how our inner battle is affecting other people.

If you're starting to see the effects your fear of rejection has had on those around you, you might have some relationships that are in need of repair. The most important part is to come to a healthy place yourself. If you believe other people are always the problem, you probably need a bit more self-awareness. Likewise, if you always take the blame and try to be the one who constantly changes to make someone else happy, you are out of balance. You can only be responsible for yourself, so learning what's in your yard and what's in someone else's is a really helpful practice.

Rejection is not something that is often addressed in society or in the church today. It is not well understood by the general public, and if it's something you haven't personally faced, you really have no grid for what it's like. Understanding rejection and social anxiety helps us know what to do with it, so someone with no grid for rejection won't have a great solution for how to fix it.

When a plumber is learning their trade, they first learn how things work properly, and then they're shown the common ways that plumbing may break or malfunction. Only then are they taught how to fix them. It is the same for us as we are going through spiritual development and facing challenges like fear and rejection. We first need to understand the proper intended function, then the specific challenges with fear and rejection. Then we can move forward into repairing what went wrong, and be restored back to health and wholeness.

Watching someone struggle with these things from the outside can be confusing and misleading. So much of our processing is done internally, so you are only seeing reactions and not the preceding triggers and progression of thoughts that lead to them.

It's like seeing someone explode with road rage when a minor inconvenience occurs. You know their overreaction must have other factors contributing to it, but from the outside it looks like this one small incident caused an extreme reaction. With the full context, you would better understand why their reaction was so extreme.

When someone is triggered by rejection, they might have one of those "fight, flight, or freeze" reactions. They could respond with anger, attacking the person who hurt them and doing their best to deliver a counter-attack. They might freeze, becoming real quiet, and from the outside it appears there is nothing going on or that they are not enjoying themselves. Or they might avoid any situation that might trigger them, turning down social invitations and skipping family obligations. Any of these behaviours taken out of context are confusing for the other people in the room.

Most of the time, we interpret other people's actions to be about us. It's so hard to imagine that something might not be about us! When we love someone who is triggered by rejection, it is really tempting to assume that all of their actions and attitudes are because of something we have done or said. It's of course good to be sensitive to what other people are going through and aware of when someone is struggling. The problem comes when we assume it's always about us, or that it is always up to us to fix.

If you don't yet know the reason they are struggling, you might be offended at the actions or attitudes of your friend. You might assume they are a grumpy person, always in a bad mood because they're just not being positive enough. You might think they don't ever want to hang out with you if they are always cancelling plans and not showing up when they say they will. Or you might wonder why they never open up and share what's really going on. Who knows how many friendships and relationships have slowly died because one person was struggling and the other person was confused about what was happening.

Most of the time, we interpret other people's actions to be about us.

One of the strategies of the enemy is to get us to misdiagnose our problems. If you've ever had a medical problem, you know that half of the solution is getting an accurate diagnosis. With rejection, it often takes quite awhile to figure out what the root of the problem is—we spend so much time thinking that our circumstances are the problem, that if other people would change we would be fine. Through that process, our closest friends and loved ones can take some of the blame and even become a crutch that we lean on, asking them to take responsibility for making us feel better. Untangling those layers of unhealthy habits takes a lot of intentional action, and will require both you and your loved ones making a change.

Vulnerability

Vulnerability is a vital tool in relationships. If we can't be open and honest about the things we are struggling with, is the friendship even worth investing in? There are appropriate levels of vulnerability in different relationships, and we should be aware of the balance. Commitment is the key to balancing out vulnerability. The things that you share with someone, the level of vulnerability you show should be equal to the level of commitment in the relationship.

When you have more vulnerability than you do commitment, you will overshare and probably feel unsafe. When you have a lot of commitment but low vulnerability, there won't be any depth to the relationship, which leads to a different aspect of feeling unsafe. Both are unhealthy, so we want to work towards that balance where we share deeper things with people who have some level of commitment to us in relationship.

If someone who is struggling with rejection opens up to you about it and shares what they are processing, recognize that that was probably a really scary thing for them to do. It's hard to talk about, and the very act of them sharing shows that they are extending you a level of trust that isn't natural for them. They have taken a risk, and the best thing you can do is honour that risk by listening. Very few people know how to listen well these days. Most people are listening with the goal of forming their reply, while true listening has nothing to do with what is said next.

True listening gives space to someone to explore and express their ideas, thoughts and emotions. A good listener will make you feel heard and not just endured. When someone opens up about something they are struggling with—whether it's rejection or something else—it honours them when you not only give them space to share, but you also ask questions to better understand their point of view.

It is tempting to want to correct wrong beliefs in other people, to jump in and help them see where they're wrong. When you see someone believing a lie, or misunderstanding an action, it is love that prompts you to show them what you see. But it is also love that holds your tongue, that gives them room and seeks to understand how they came to be where they are. Listening and understanding will create a culture of vulnerability in all your relationships, and allow you to be the safe person that others can share with. You can and should still speak the truth, but first give them space to express where they're at.

Boundaries

Fixing other people is not your job. Healing other people is not your job (unless you're a doctor). Correcting other people is not your job (unless you have authority over them). We can be so motivated by love, but a poor application of love will do more damage than good. Don't turn off your love; don't become jaded; don't stop helping others. But the balance here is in knowing what love looks like in each situation. This is why partnering with the Holy Spirit is so important, and we want to be sensitive to hear what God is saying about every area of our lives, including relationships where people are struggling.

When I was going through some of the worst seasons of rejection in my life, I had a dear friend who was trying to love me through it. She wanted to wave a magic wand and fix it all. She saw my pain, saw that I was stuck in a cycle of rejection and that I didn't know how to get out. I can only imagine what it was like to be my friend during that time...It wasn't all bad—we had a lot of great experiences together, but I'm sure it was confusing to see me disappear or go from fine to extremely not fine at the drop of a hat.

One night this friend of mine had a dream, and in her dream, I was standing on the other side of a glass door and I was on the phone. I was clearly upset, and she wanted to come outside and help me. She didn't know what I was upset about, but she saw me hurting and wanted to fix it. In the dream, the Lord wouldn't let her open the door. He locked it, and told her that He was the One who was on the phone with me. He asked her to let Him be the One to fix it, to trust Him with me and with my pain. He was showing her what love looked like, and at that time it looked like taking a step back.

This might sound cold and like a negative point of view. It is counter intuitive to take a step back when someone you love is hurting. But in this case, at this time, that is what love looked like. I needed to be "on the phone" with God, to be communicating with Him directly so He could teach me all the things I'm sharing with you in this book. He needed to be the One to lead me out of that desert into my promised land, and in this dream, He was reassuring my friend that He was on it. When it feels like nothing you are doing is helping, take a step back and pray. Hear from God about what is happening, and ask Him what love looks like— at *this* time and with *this* person.

Boundaries are not a one size fits all solution; they are so much more about the heart posture than the action. After my friend had that dream, there wasn't a whole lot that changed outwardly. I didn't feel her pull away and she didn't do a lot differently in our day-to-day life. It was more about her heart—all the pressure was off her to fix me.

She no longer tried to correct every belief I had or took responsibility for my mood and involvement in every social situation. What is going on in our hearts matters enormously to the Lord, and in His kindness, He will bring correction when we need it. If you have a friend or loved one who is struggling with rejection, this might be the biggest area that needs to change: your own heart.

Let go of all pressure you've taken on to make things better for them. Shake off the responsibility to keep them happy. Tear down any beliefs you have that it is your job to get them fixed. We will always fail if we are working harder on someone's problems than they are willing to themselves. Any responsibility that you take away from someone else is authority that you are robbing them of. That is not love.

If you do your teenager's homework for them, say it's a science project and you swoop in and take it over so that it's done right. When they get an award for that project, they have no authority to receive or celebrate that award—you've robbed them of that. They also won't have any idea of how to recreate it in the future when they need to. We need to let our loved ones who are dealing with rejection take hold of the victory for themselves so that they can continue to walk it out in all of their relationships.

Supporting someone doesn't mean you're fixing their problems; it means you love them where they're at. Allow them to be broken, to be imperfect, to have emotions and reactions. Most people don't have a safe place to express what's going on inside of them, and if you can be a safe place for them to process without taking responsibility for fixing it, you will be a rare and helpful refuge for your friend.

What I'm describing sounds lovely, but in practice is actually quite difficult. It requires setting aside your own desires and natural inclination to help. If someone is stuck in this cycle of being triggered by rejection, your learning more about it is a really helpful thing. Ask questions; read about it; think about your own rejection experiences and how you process them. Sometimes it can feel really lonely, and if you can relate, it builds a great connection.

One of the best ways to be a friend to someone who is struggling is by being really healthy yourself. Simply living a life that is free of the fear of rejection and modelling that in quiet ways is a beautiful sign to your friend that it is possible to live in freedom. When we're stuck, it's often because we don't know what freedom would even look like. Share with your friend your thought process when you are rejected or feel afraid.

When your loved one is going through the process of healing, when they are doing the work to renew their minds and using the tools in this book to live in victory over rejection, you can support them is by letting them lead. Let them be responsible for what that healing process looks like. Ask them what would be helpful.

They might have specific phrases or thoughts that they are working on, and you being on the same page will be a great resource. Wait for a time when they are feeling good, and ask them what would be helpful for you to do or say the next time they feel triggered. As long as they're not asking you to do the work for them, you repeating the same message that they've figured out they need to focus on will be a great help.

Supporting someone doesn't mean you're fixing their problems; it means you love them where they're at.

The bottom line is you want to support them without doing the work for them. Speak the truth with lots of grace, and work with them to find language that is helpful. It is a fine line between being supportive while not agreeing with the lies that have taken root, but it's a line worth finding. Someone who is fighting a fear of rejection has a narrative in their head that might often be about you, but the root of it is not about you at all. If they come to you with accusations about ways you have rejected them and hurt their feelings, pause before you respond.

An important thing to note is that rejection can be intentional or perceived, and the effects are the same. Intentional rejection is when there is a conscious choice to reject someone, whether in a small way or a more permanent rejection (it may or may not have had a malicious intent). Perceived rejection is when the person interprets a word or action as rejection when there was no intent towards that. Either one has a real consequence—just because you didn't mean to reject them doesn't mean their feelings in response are invalid.

Telling someone their response, their feelings, and their experience are not valid can be really damaging. Denying someone their experience is not actually helpful, even if your point is true. You can assure them of your intention and clarify your point of view, but don't shut down their experience. Even feelings that are triggered by a lie are still feelings that need to be dealt with.

If there are ways that you have rejected them intentionally, own it! There might be small ways you have needed some distance or created some boundaries because of your own needs, which felt like rejection to someone else. Instead of denying those things, take time to explain your motivation and why you made those choices. You don't need to apologize for every decision you make, but explaining the reasons you made those decisions can be really helpful. Remind the person who struggles with a fear of rejection that it is not all about them.

Codependency

It is really common for people who struggle with rejection to enter a codependent relationship with a loved one. This might be a spouse, a friend, or a family member. When one person is always caretaking and the other is relying on them to take care of their needs, an unhealthy dynamic is prevalent. With rejection, this often shows up as one person needing the other one to regulate their mood—if the caretaker doesn't show up in a certain way, the other will emotionally break down. There is not one person to blame in a codependent relationship, each one is getting a need met by either being saved or being the one who saves. Both are unhealthy, and both people need to make a change.

The good news is that change is not only possible, it is God's design. This is not an unnatural shift; it is a return to the intended function of your relationship. Sometimes, in extreme and long-term cases, a break is needed for both parties to become healthy. But more often than not, the change can be made while maintaining a relationship.

This is why we need intimacy with the Holy Spirit, because He is a genius at relationships and knows exactly what is needed for each time and person. Take time to hear from God about what is needed to create a healthy relationship. To change the codependent dynamic, each person needs to go through their own process with the Lord. All the tools given in this book—repentance, forgiveness, and renewing your mind—will be helpful as each of you navigate those changes. Take responsibility for your part, and let the other person be responsible for theirs.

If you have been showing up as the saviour and regulating the emotions of the other person, you will need to practice some new boundaries. You might need to create a bit of distance and not be physically available as often as they would like. You might need to change your language and not apologize for what has caused rejection so often. You might need to instead explain some of your thoughts and perspective instead of agreeing with the narrative presented to you.

There might be some really practical changes you make in your relationship, and the best thing you can do is communicate clearly. Let your loved one know what they can expect from you moving forward, and why you are making these changes. Assure them of your continued love for them, and explain how love might look different in the future than it has in the past.

Codependency is a dangerous habit because it always gives power and authority where it is not meant to be. God is the One who should have that level of influence in our lives, and when we give it to another human being, we are on dangerous ground. We want Him to be the One who has the role of Saviour, the One who is our source for joy and peace, and the One whose words and opinions matter above anyone else. We don't want to give someone else that role, and we definitely don't want to take on that role for someone else. It is rebellion either way, and we need to guard against that.

Love Looks Like Something

If you love someone who is struggling with fear, rejection, and/or social anxiety, you have likely felt the ups and downs of that journey with them. Freedom is possible, and they might look a little different when they're free. One of the hardest things to do is to allow people to change, even when it's a positive change. We tend to hold on to the stories and the patterns, and get uncomfortable with any kind of change in our lives. When someone close to you is growing, they will grow imperfectly. Have some grace for them, and for yourself through the process. Continually evaluate your expectations, and if you find that you are always expecting them to always be triggered and to react a certain way, recognize that you may be encouraging it through your words and actions.

When you see your friend starting to change, release them from your expectations. Allow them to grow by removing the limits that seemed necessary before. Extend invitations that have been turned down in the past. Ask questions about how they are experiencing the world. Try not to make comments that pin them down as the person they used to be.

You might find that you need to get to know them all over again, and that can be a really fun thing! We should always be asking: what does love look like, with this person, at this time. There are no formulas for love, but the connection found on the other side of this process is worth the discomfort of walking it out together.

This intentional love can be difficult and require a lot of energy. This will be incredibly draining if you are not connected to God, the source of love itself. Make sure you are cultivating a lifestyle that allows you to spend time in His presence and to regularly fill up so that you have enough to give away. Protect that time with the Lord and learn what things help you connect with Him. The best friend is a healthy friend, and often the best way you can love the people around you is to first receive love yourself.

11

Loving Well

The sneaky agenda of rejection is not just about what it does to you, but it's also about how it affects the people around you. Its goal is one of two outcomes: either to isolate you or to decay your relationships until there's no love left in them. This is the endgame of rejection, and it won't stop until that happens.

It stands to reason then, that someone living in victory over rejection has healthy, loving relationships. They are connected, secure and able to maintain healthy boundaries. When people are living in victory over rejection, it means rejection and everything that follows after it is under their feet. They are literally living over it, above it, secure in their authority. It's not that rejection ceases to exist, but it ceases to have any power or influence over you. You are the head and not the tail. This is the great freedom that is afforded to us by the cross: that our enemy is now under our feet because of the authority of Christ. This is not a victory we are waiting for until we are in heaven; it is part of our reality here and now.

When we talk about the Kingdom of heaven, we talk about the now and not yet—the mystery of living on earth in between the resurrection of Christ and His return in the last days. We attempt to explain that in between season by pushing the benefits of heaven forward into the future to explain the brokenness of our current reality. The danger of that, however, is that we fail to take hold of the victory of the cross, its benefits, and the inheritance that God has provided for us here and now in the midst of a broken world.

The reality is, Jesus Himself instructed us to pray that things would be on earth as they are in heaven. He could have told us to pray, "Lord give us strength and patience to wait for the victory we will see in heaven" but He didn't! He gave us the boldness to pray, "on earth as it is in heaven," because it's actually possible.

Jesus didn't give impossible directives; He gave directives that were impossible for us to do on our own. He asked us to do things that we could only do with His help, and this prayer is one of them. Our victory does not depend on our performance, our gifts, or our maturity. Our victory rests squarely on His shoulders, and was fully paid for more than two thousand years ago.

My own victory over rejection did not come after I followed the right formula or said the right prayers. My victory came when I realized that God's love was so much more powerful than any rejection I could ever face.

His authority is so complete that even though I had opened the door for the enemy in my life through offense, bitterness, judgement, unforgiveness, pride, and many other things, I could close all of those doors simply because Jesus paid the price for me. God's grace is so vast that it covers my own mistakes, as well as the mistakes of everyone who has hurt and rejected me. His love is so powerful that everything that has been stolen from me by rejection, fear, and anxiety has been restored just through the Presence of the Holy Spirit.

My victory did not come through changed circumstances. We have got to get our hope off of our circumstances and on to the One who is the very essence of hope itself. I am still a person who has been rejected. I am still single; I have not been given jobs to replace the ones I lost, and I have not seen every old relationship reconciled. I am not writing to you from a place of "Everything is better!" I am writing to you with the message that "God will meet you right where you are!" When I say that what was stolen has been restored, I am talking about the pieces of me that were stolen.

Jesus didn't give impossible directives; He gave directives that were impossible for us to do on our own.

The longer you live on this earth, the more you realize what is truly valuable, what is truly worth protecting. For me, that is fruit. Fruit is incredibly valuable to me. Living in the Okanagan here in Canada, we do summer fruit really well. Peaches and cherries fresh picked and warm from the sun: this is summer to me. You'll see fruit stands across highways well into the prairies selling "BC cherries"—some hard-working men and women who have picked the fruit and driven it all the way across highway 1 to sell it to the hungry flat landers. Now, living here, I know I can get a bucket of cherries for free from my neighbours. But those people a few provinces away, they are paying a hefty fee for that same bucket.

The value is demonstrated in the abundance of the fruit. When fruit is overflowing, you'll get it for free. When there are only a few available, you'll pay a high price for them.

This is how it works with the fruit of the Spirit. When you have a scarce amount of love, it is costly to give it away. When you are overflowing, the people next to you are going to take some for free; you won't even notice what's missing. The same is true for joy, peace, patience, kindness, goodness, faithfulness, gentleness and self-control.

You are probably familiar with this passage of Scripture, the fruit of the Spirit found in Galatians. Paul wrote this book to the church in southern Galatia—he had helped establish this community of believers about 2 years earlier and was writing to help them grow into maturity. He was teaching them about love, how important it was for them to cultivate and what it looks like when a community of believers puts love into practice.

> *"But the fruit of the Spirit is love, joy, peace, patience, kindness, goodness, faithfulness, gentleness, self-control; against such things there is no law."*

> *Galatians 5:22-23*

We are used to reading this passage as a list of different kinds of fruit—a basket of different good things the Spirit produces. But there's actually a small grammatical distinction that could change our perspective of this familiar passage. Some scholars believe that at the very beginning of that verse is a colon, and it should read like this.

> *"But the fruit of the Spirit is love: joy, peace, patience, kindness, goodness, faithfulness, gentleness, self-control; against such things there is no law."*

Do you see the difference? If that was intended to be a description rather than a list, it helps us understand how to love each other well. Because there was very little punctuation in the original Greek manuscripts, we can't be sure whether that should be a comma or a colon, but either way we read it we are learning about love.

Paul is teaching them, and us, what love looks like. Love looks like patience. Love looks like self-control. The fruit of the Spirit is love. The rest is an explainer for those of us who need a reminder of what love looks like. We think that when we're low on patience we need to ask God for more patience, but what we really need is more love. We believe that if we're lacking self-control we have other problems, but what we really have is a love problem. There is one giant, beautiful piece of fruit in that basket, and it is love.

How do we apply this truth, how do we love other people well? We want to have all of these things in our relationships—joy, peace, patience, kindness, goodness, faithfulness, gentleness and self-control. But focusing on those things themselves won't help us accomplish them.

They are the product of love, the natural outcome of having received love ourselves. We can only produce this outcome when we have been loved and understand what love is. Allowing ourselves to be loved is the best way to become great at giving love. If you want to be a more patient person, you need to let love touch the parts of you that are lacking in patience. The problem is, there is no human who is capable of loving you enough. We are all messy and carrying our own wounds and needs, and even with the best intentions and the healthiest families, we still make mistakes and have limited capacities.

In order to be able to love other messy humans well, we need a source for love that doesn't have the same limitations. If we want to cultivate the fruit of love in our lives, we have to set aside other agendas for our relationships. If we are looking to other people to make us feel secure, to tell us who we are, to give approval or acceptance, we have an ulterior motive that is conflicting with the agenda of love. We are not free to love people if we are waiting for them to approve of us.

We are free to love when we already have those needs met by the One who created us. We must look to the Lord and allow Him to provide security and fill us with love so that we are free to love the people around us. I love reading about Jesus being tempted in the wilderness because we get great insight into how the enemy tempts us and what victory looks like.

This narrative is found in Matthew 4, and if you'll allow me to summarize for you, Jesus while fasting, is led by the Spirit into the wilderness for a time of temptation. I don't know about you, but when I'm fasting, I am more vulnerable and easily tempted. The enemy approaches Jesus three different ways, with three different lies for Him to consider.

The first one is centered around provision. He is tempting Him with the lie that He will go hungry and the Father won't provide for Him. Remember, Jesus is fasting, and the enemy encourages Him to turn stone into bread so that He can eat. Jesus answered by declaring a truth out loud.

The second lie suggested to Jesus is that the Father won't protect Him. He's asking Jesus to prove that even if He throws Himself off a high place the angels will keep Him from harm. Again, Jesus answers by declaring a truth out loud.

Thirdly, the enemy tempts Jesus with a lie around acceptance and approval. He offers Him all the glory from the kingdoms of this world. Finally, Jesus commands the enemy to leave and again declares a truth out loud.

It's interesting that Jesus doesn't get caught in logical arguments, debating the facts with the enemy. He just states the truth out loud, and moves on. There's a lot of "keyboard warriors" in our day today that would do well to notice that strategy.

Provision, protection and approval—these are the three areas that Jesus is tempted in and the three areas that He demonstrates victory over. We tend to think of temptation in the terms of violent sins and actions—and yet the one recorded narrative we have about Jesus facing temptation is surrounding lies about who God would be for Him. Our greatest temptations are the ones that take place only in our thoughts, the ones that we can justify with our circumstances. The way Jesus exercised His victory was by declaring truth out loud and rebuking the enemy. For each of us, there are likely lies around these core beliefs that we must gain victory over.

Being a child of God means that we are inherently provided for, protected, and approved of by a loving Father. You cannot separate a child of God from the love of God. A child being protected and provided for does not actually depend on the child at all, it is 100% the responsibility of the Father. Provision, protection, and approval are not conditional benefits; they are the very character of our heavenly Father.

If it is true for one of us, then it's true for all of us. You are not so special that you are the one child of God that will not be provided for, protected, or approved of! When we don't have this assurance, when we are tempted by the lies of the enemy. We either live in fear that we don't have any protection, provision, and approval—or we look to someone else to meet those needs instead of God.

That's why rejection can be so devastating—when we are needing approval and get rejected our very foundation is shaken. But when we have assurance of our approval from the Father, rejection from someone else is not so disruptive. It still hurts, yes, but it does not affect our foundation.

This is why so many of our relational problems actually have nothing to do with other people. Most of the time, we are lacking an understanding of God's love for us, and when we focus on increasing our connection with the Father and accepting His love for us, we see exponential breakthrough in our other relationships. Cultivating intimacy with the Lord is a necessary way of life if you want to have enough love to give away to others. This is where the fruit of the Spirit comes from, from: our connection with the Lord. The more we understand how loved we are, the more love we have to give away. It is one area of life wherein trying harder only pushes you further away from your goal. Rest and receive—this is how you get closer to your goal of loving people well.

When I was going through my healing process, I didn't know much about love. I wanted to be good at loving people, but I found it difficult. Love felt really unsafe. As God worked on my healing, He was gentle and kind enough to take it slow with me. It would have been too much to go from 0 to 60 right away. That's the great thing about the Holy Spirit: He is not into formulas. He knows our unique strengths and weaknesses, our quirks and personalities and history. He knows the exact keys and process that is needed to bring the fullness of healing that we require. For me, He knew that I needed a few gradual steps as I grew in love.

At the time, the first safe step I took was accepting God's love for me. I couldn't go anywhere or expand my horizons at all until I took that step. I acknowledged the truth of His love for me and repented for believing otherwise. I let His love become personal, not just accepting a general premise that He is a loving God who loves people, but that He actually loves me. I persisted through the discomfort of being seen by another, being fully known, and allowed Him to love me. I stopped hiding parts of myself from Him and became brutally honest and vulnerable.

The next safest step for me was loving a puppy. I'm not kidding—the Lord knew that people were still scary for me, so the love of a puppy was my next benchmark. I only had her for a brief time, but Penny was the cutest little beagle you have ever seen. Her floppy velvet ears, her tiny tongue that would excitedly lick my salty tears as I worked through grief, growth, and pain. As silly as it sounds, allowing myself to love and be loved by this energetic puppy was a necessary step ordained by God.

Next, I was ready for the scariest thing: actual human love. But still, God's kindness provided for me. I had a daycare at the time, a collection of seven kids ages 1-4 that would invade my home every day with all of their reasonable immaturity. This was my next benchmark, allowing myself to love and be loved by babies and toddlers. As I learned and grew in love, I saw how vital it was to stay connected to Love Himself in order to love others. When I found myself running low on patience, I asked God to love me. This was a great training ground for me, and I'm incredibly grateful for the years that I spent in that little red house on Pleasant Valley Road.

I should add here that at the time, I didn't understand why that season was taking so long. I had a vision for my life that extended beyond that home and that daycare, but there was no grace to make a change that aligned with my vision. Looking back now, I can see that God was keeping me in that place to allow me to practice and grow in love in a safe, stable way. We often want to rush through seasons and fast-forward, not understanding that it is a gift that God is trying to give us. If I could go back, I would be content in the waiting. I would trust that God's timing was actually an expression of His love.

After my season with the daycare ended, God released me to start loving people. Actual human grownups, with all their reasonable immaturity. This part felt like getting thrown into the deep end—people with their own free will and shortcomings and mistakes. But the principles I had learned in my training ground still served me in the deep end.

When I felt low on patience or gentleness or self-control, I ran to the Father and let Him love me. It is counter-intuitive but profoundly productive—we think when we are lacking fruit that we need to love better, but what we really need is to be loved. Quite often the best use of your time is to "waste" it at the feet of Jesus. Don't leave your home in the morning until you know how loved you are. Don't even leave your bed until you are aware of God's love for you. This one habit will change your life.

I haven't done it perfectly (none of us do), but this is what I am growing in. Learning to identify when a part of me is feeling unloved, unseen, or rejected, and bringing that piece of me to Jesus before I bring it to someone else. It is not so much a formula as it is a heart posture. This is not an item on your to do list; it is a lifestyle of intimacy.

When this becomes natural you will have a secure foundation and solid ground that you can stand on and begin to love other people well. It is surprising how little energy it takes to love other people when you have this foundation. What feels exhausting when you are mustering it up on your own feels easy when you are allowing God to be your source and are receiving from Him.

Being loved well by God also helps us to have healthy boundaries. When we are secure in love, we don't need other people to meet our needs, fix our problems, or make us feel better. Most of our habits of poor boundaries stem from a desire to control what's happening around us—we want to make sure other people are happy, or we want to make other people like us, or we want to try to stop bad things from happening.

In very general terms, that is why we lack boundaries and allow other people to have roles and responsibilities that they were never meant to have. All of this need for control and people-pleasing is rooted in fear, and fear is in opposition to love. The areas in which we are afraid are the areas we have not allowed ourselves to be loved by God. It sounds like an oversimplification, but when we start to apply this, we see incredible breakthrough.

Let's break it down into a small example. I might have poor boundaries at work, giving up breaks and working overtime and holidays to meet goals or make progress. If I want approval from other people, I might start working so hard that I sacrifice my own personal health in order to be recognized at work or school for my efforts. This could lead to physical and mental health problems, lost relationships and eventual burnout and breakdown, all in an effort to be accepted. All of this looks different when I stop and let God love me.

When I allow God to see the ugliest parts of me and get nothing but love in return, I build a strong foundation of acceptance in His love. When that is established, I don't need to earn approval through my work or performance, and I can contribute to my job with a healthy boundary. I can recognize my own limitations and leave work without needing to be everything to everybody. I know I'll survive if and when mistakes happen, because I have that foundation and security of God's constant love even on my worst day. Healthy boundaries are a natural outcome of a well-loved person.

You are able to love people well when you are well loved. Waiting for other messy humans to love you well is a painful game. It's time we stop striving, stop trying to earn what has already been paid in full—we love because He first loved us. Loving people well is not about making other people feel good, although that is a great outcome. Loving people well is actually about being the healthiest version of ourselves we can be, and that is what happens when we allow God to love us.

There will still be messes. There will still be mistakes. There will still be days when you wonder why you bother trying. But it's worth it; this whole journey is worth it to get even a little bit closer to resembling our Father.

I completed the School of Biblical Studies a few years ago

with YWAM (Youth With A Mission). Through this intensive program, we read through the entire Bible at least 5 times, in 5 different ways. I loved it, and I still love my Bible and the life that it brings. There are so many passages that are special to me, but if I had to pick, I would say that Romans 8 is my favourite chapter in all of Scripture. This passage sums up an important principle for us to grasp as we walk out our victory over rejection.

> *"For all who are led by the Spirit of God are sons of God. For you did not receive the spirit of slavery to fall back into fear, but you have received the Spirit of adoption as sons, by whom we cry, Abba! Father! The Spirit himself bears witness with our spirit that we are children of God, and if children, then heirs—heirs of God and fellow heirs with Christ, provided we suffer with him in order that we may also be glorified with him."*

Romans 8:14-17

This is the key that each of us needs to have planted within us: we have been adopted. Whatever ways you have been rejected and hurt in your lifetime, none of that reduces or diminishes the truth that you have been chosen and adopted by God. Christ is your fellow heir, the Holy Spirit is your inheritance, and you legally have all the same rights as any child of God does. There is nothing that can separate you from this truth.

There is a contrast here between a spirit of slavery (fear) and a spirit of adoption. They cannot both be true because they are opposed to each other. If you believe that you have been adopted into the family of God, you have to let go of the voice of fear and rejection.

You are absolutely worthy of being loved well. I am sorry for all the times you have been hurt. I'm sorry for the times you have been overlooked, bullied, or forgotten. I'm sorry for all the ways you were mistreated and cast aside. I'm sorry for how you have been rejected. I see you. I see your value, I see your beauty, I see your brilliance. You are worthy of being fully known and fully accepted.

There is no part of your past, present or future that is not covered by the love of God. Every wound, every tear, every heartache—none of it is wasted. Every piece of your past is redeemed by the blood of Jesus and every mistake is forgiven. Everything that was stolen from you is restored by His love. Every lost hope is being strengthened; every lost year is being returned. Every fear is uprooted and every hope is made whole in His Presence. You cannot begin to fathom the freedom that you are stepping in to as you take hold of victory over rejection. All of heaven is cheering you on.

ABOUT THE AUTHOR

Amy Hayward is a Canadian author and speaker. Born in Winnipeg, Manitoba and currently living in Redding, CA, she also spent a good part of her life and ministry in Vernon, BC. She has a passion for seeing the church across North America embrace the beautiful symmetry of the Holy Spirit and the Word of God, and to be an example to the world of what it looks like to love one another and fulfill the mandate Jesus gave us in John 13:35. After graduating with the School of Biblical Studies through Youth With A Mission, Amy has been attending Bethel School of Supernatural Ministry. She has worked in ministry for twenty years and loves encouraging and equipping people to hear God and find inner healing. Visit her online to find the Speak Beloved Podcast, E-courses and more.

SPEAK BELOVED PODCAST

Speak Beloved has been a blog since 2013, a place where I have shared encouragement for people on a journey of faith. It's where I have explored the Scriptures and words I have received that have been a catalyst for transformation in my life. The name, Speak Beloved was significant for me as I accepted my identity as God's beloved. Now more than ever each of us should know that our voice is counted, it's needed, it's vital that we raise our voices as God's beloved in this world, speaking truth with clarity. If you appreciate podcasts, I hope you will find this one encouraging. Thank you for listening, for sharing, for rating and reviewing. You can expect a 20 minute episode every other week, with topics about hearing God, and applying what we hear.

DREAMING WITH GOD E-COURSE

Dreaming with God is a fun, dynamic process that can release revelation, direction and encouragement in a unique way. Anyone can hear from God through their dreams, and become confident in interpreting them. In this course, we will explore the purpose for dreams, basic principles of interpretation, and how to apply and steward the dreams God gives you. You'll have the confidence to interpret your dreams and see explosive growth in your intimacy with the Lord!

- PURPOSE OF DREAMS
- LEARNING THE LANGUAGE OF HEAVEN
- PROCESSING DIFFERENT TYPES OF DREAMS
- INTERPRETING SYMBOLS, COLOUR AND NUMBERS
- STEWARDING YOUR DREAMS
- ACTIVATION

VICTORY OVER REJECTION E-COURSE

Take the Victory Over Rejection E-course at speakbeloved.com to make the most out of the content in this book. In a series of short videos, author Amy Hayward will personally lead you through the application of the tools that are included in the book. This e-course is for anyone who has been struggling with rejection and wants to take the time to make sure they are implementing the truth, that we already have victory over rejection because of Jesus Christ and His work on the cross. Freedom is available!

Manufactured by Amazon.ca
Bolton, ON

29435145R00096